D1522609

The
Population
Challenge

CONTRIBUTIONS IN SOCIOLOGY

Series Editor: Don Martindale

Johannes Overbeek

THE
POPULATION
CHALLENGE

A handbook for nonspecialists

Contributions in Sociology, Number 19

GREENWOOD PRESS
Westport, Connecticut • *London, England*

Library of Congress Cataloging in Publication Data

Overbeek, Johannes.
  The population challenge.

  (Contributions in sociology; no. 19)
  Bibliography: p.
  Includes index.
  1. Population. 2. Population policy. I. Title.
HB871.093 1976   301.32   76-5328
ISBN 0-8371-8896-2

Library of Congress Catalog Card Number: 76-5328
ISBN: 0-8371-8896-2

First published in 1976

Greenwood Press, a division of Williamhouse-Regency Inc.
51 Riverside Avenue, Westport, Connecticut 06880

Manufactured in the United States of America

TO CHANTAL

CONTENTS

LIST OF TABLES

LIST OF FIGURES

Preface

At the annual meeting of the Population Association of America in April 1975, several speakers observed that the United Nations World Population Conference held in Bucharest (August 1974) received mediocre coverage in the American press. The manner in which journalists and laymen reacted to the conclusions of the conference showed that even now population matters are ill understood by the general public and press, especially when such issues reach a certain level of complexity. The need for more efforts to educate the public in this area was clearly recognized.

This book, then, attempts to explain in simple terms some basic facts about population with special emphasis on the causes and consequences of the present trends in population. Population policy is also given due attention. At the risk of seeming pedantic, I have made incursions into fields of knowledge outside my own area of specialization. An interdisciplinary topic such as population seems to make this unavoidable.

I have made a considerable effort to give a truly objective account and have avoided the crisis perspective as much as possible. The publications of the alarmists may have a salutary "shake-up" effect on the public, but the danger is a one-sided presentation of facts and data, while apocalyptic visions may actually paralyze action altogether. Yet optimism just for the good feeling it creates is a luxury mankind can ill afford at this point.

In writing this book I have drawn freely on the existing body of scholarship. I was lucky enough to be surrounded and assisted by the highly qualified and able team of the East-West Population Institute directed by Dr. Lee-Jay Cho.

I received a great deal of help, for which I am extremely grateful. James Saunders carefully edited the manuscript and is entitled to my sincerest thanks. Dr. Fred Hung read the entire work and made many suggestions for improvement. I further greatly benefited from the advice and assistance of Dr. Fred Pope, Dr. Robert Retherford, Dr. Robert Gardner, Dr. Dennis Chao, Mrs. Eleanor Nordyke, and Mrs. Alice Harris. Mr. Everett Wingert drew the graphs and Miss Violenda Kipapa typed and retyped the manuscript with admirable patience. Mahalo! Needless to say, should any errors remain, both the blame and the responsibility are mine.

The Population Challenge

1

The growth of population

Be fruitful, and multiply, and replenish the earth.

Genesis 1:28

Demographic Inflation

There is common agreement among optimists and pessimists that the contemporary growth of the world population is revolutionary, to say the least. It is probably safe to say also that the present fast growth of the human race cannot continue for long, because at present rates of growth the whole land area of the world will have become one giant city in only 300 years. In 700 to 800 years, standing room only will be the rule over the entire face of the earth, and in some 8,000 years the whole astronomical universe will be packed solid with human flesh.

To get an idea of the unusual speed at which the human flood is rising, it is useful to begin with a bird's eye view of population and growth in the past. It is estimated that in 8000 B.C. there were 10 million people on earth; in 3500 B.C., perhaps around 30 million. At the birth of Christ the planet's population stood at some 300 million. Between the birth of Christ and the year 1800, population grew to 1 billion. Only 130 years later (in 1930) the 2 billion figure was reached. Some thirty years later (around 1960) the 3 billion figure

Table 1. *Estimates of World Population by Region, 1650 to 2000*[a]
(In millions)

	1650	1750	1800	1850	1900	1950	1970	1990	2000
World total	545	728	906	1,171	1,608	2,400	3,632	5,438	6,494
Europe	100	140	187	266	401	541[b]	462	533	568
North America	1	1.3	5.7	26	81	166	228	299	333
Latin America	12	11.1	18.9	33	63	162	283	500	652
Russia USSR	15					195	243	302	330
Asia	330	479	602	749	937	1,320	2,056	3,177	3,778
Africa	100	95	90	95	120	198	344	616	818
Oceania	2	2	2	2	6	13	19	30	35

[a]*The estimates for the period after 1950 are based on the medium fertility variant as used by the United Nations Statistical Office.*

[b]*Until 1950 the figures for Europe include the population of the European part of the USSR; after 1950 they exclude the Soviet Russian population.*

was recorded; and in 1975, fifteen years later, the estimate was 4 billion people on earth. Approximately ten years later, in 1985 or 1986, the 5 billion figure will be reached. The broad facts of population growth between 1650 and 2000 are made clear by Table 1.

Presently (1974) world population is increasing by a figure of about 80 million per annum. The larger part of this annual growth takes place in the nonindustrialized, low-income countries, as Table 2 shows. What will happen in the near future is less predictable, of course; but the most reliable estimates tell us that by the year 2000, world population will have grown to a low 6.129 billion or a high 7.5 billion. Figure 1 illustrates the growth from the time Christ was born to the end of the twentieth century.

Figure 2 shows population growth in the United States since 1770. The population reached the 100 million mark in 1918, and 200 million in 1968. Figure 3 shows that, given an average of three children per family, it will reach 300 million before the end of this century, and 400 million by the year 2014. With an average of two children per family, the 300 million figure will be reached around 2020.

The same story of this historically unique population growth and its constant acceleration emerges from a study of the quickening rate of increase, which is found by subtracting the birthrate from the

Table 2. *Annual Increment in Population in the Year 1973*

AREA	MILLIONS
World	77
Low-income areas	69
High-income areas	8
Asia	51
Africa	9.4
Latin America	8.6
Europe	3.3
USSR	2.5
North America	1.8
Oceania	0.4

death rate allowing for net migration, and can be expressed in a percentage figure, a population with twenty deaths and eight births per thousand inhabitants giving a rate of increase of 12 per thousand or 1.2 percent.

We know little about the some 900,000 years of human history that lie behind the 6,000 years of recorded history; but it is generally

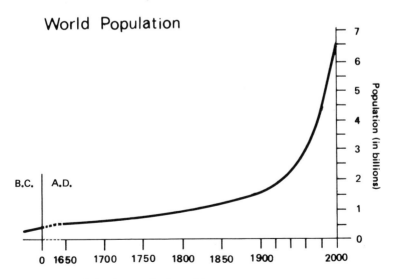

Figure 1. *Population increase in the world.*

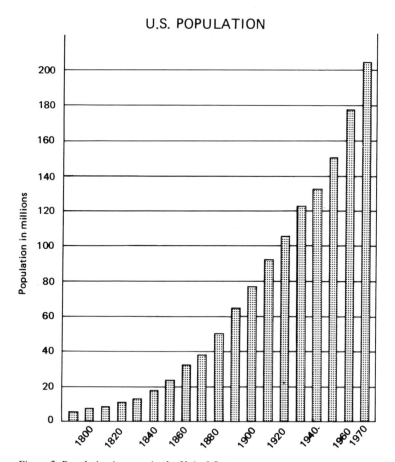

Figure 2. *Population increase in the United States.*

accepted that over the first 2,000-year period, population must have been more or less stationary. Any periods of growth that existed were followed by long periods of either stability or decline. Between the birth of Christ and the year 1500 A.D. the average annual rate of increase must have been around 0.07 percent. Table 3 tells the rest of the story.

Regional differences in growth rates are substantial. In 1972 the growth rate of the United States was estimated at 1 percent. In such

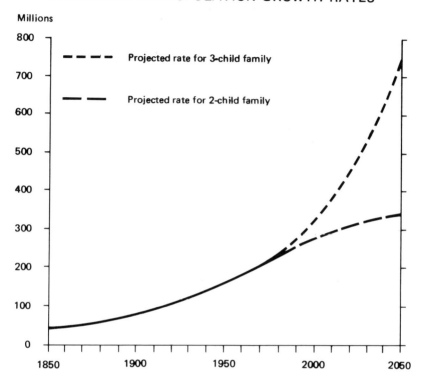

PROJECTED U.S. POPULATION GROWTH RATES

Millions

Projected rate for 3-child family

Projected rate for 2-child family

Figure 3. U.S. population growth; two-child versus three-child family. These projections assume unchanged immigration levels and a mild decline in mortality.

countries as Belgium, Austria, and West Germany it was at a low 0.2 percent, whereas in such nations as Morocco and Mexico the growth rates were respectively 3.4 percent and 3.3 percent. In the typical more developed high-income country the rate of increase is 1 percent or less, whereas in the typical less developed low-income region it is 2 to 4 percent. (To find the time it takes for a population to double, divide the growth rate into 69 or 70; thus, with a growth rate of 3 percent a population would double every 23 years.) In other words the distribution of the population increase is such that most of it takes place in the less developed countries where because of low incomes the increases are most damaging.

Table 3. *Annual Population Increase in the World*
(Based on medium U.N. projections)

YEARS	AVERAGE ANNUAL RATE OF INCREASE (%)
1500-1779	0.2
1800-1849	0.5
1850-1899	0.5
1900-1949	0.8
1950-1964	1.8
1965-1969	2.0
1970-1974	2.0
1975-1979	2.1
1980-1984	2.0
1985-1990	1.9

Taking all more developed countries together, the rate of increase is estimated to decline from the 1 percent figure in the 1970 to 1975 period to about 0.8 percent in the years 1995 to 2000. The average rate of natural increase in the low-income countries is estimated to drop from 2.5 percent in the 1970 to 1975 period to 2 percent in the years 1995 to 2000.

Origins of Demographic Inflation

The main reason for the acceleration of population growth—dramatized in the phrase "population explosion"—is, it seems, the constant decline in the death rate and the gradual improvements in health conditions that became striking after about 1750.

The fast population growth should not be attributed to some revolutionary force that had raised the birthrate.

A declining death rate and better health conditions accomplish three things. First, the probability that a pregnant woman who has conceived brings the fetus to term increases. Second, the proportion of babies who survive to the age of reproduction is raised. Finally the probability of widowhood during the reproductive period declines. All three of these circumstances enhance fertility.

Throughout human history life has been mostly cheap. Famine, disease, and war were accepted as the inevitable destroyers of human life. Death rates were fantastically high by modern standards, and life expectation at birth was low, perhaps about twenty-five years in good, and less in bad, times. Again, life was as carelessly created as it was destroyed. Unrestrained procreation and wasteful mortality were the rule; birthrates and death rates were both high, and often they nearly balanced. It may be added here that when life is short and uncertain, as throughout most of man's history, a specific mentality is its proper accompaniment; this mentality is embodied in the command to be fruitful and multiply that is to be found in many religions—an obvious relic of the life-losing past.

It may also be noted that any species, even the human, which has survived to present times must inherit a fecundity built to cope with the worst life-destroying conditions. In our present easier circumstances such fecundity is clearly excessive. Many sociologists, economists, demographers, and other students of population correctly assume that most of the growth of the human race up to say the eighteenth century or so occurred because the various inventions that made expansion of food supplies possible were inevitably followed by increases in numbers. Some eighteenth-century French writers have summed up this situation in the statement that men multiply like rats in a barn: the more wheat, the more rats.

It has been estimated that if man had remained a food gatherer living on nuts, fruits, roots, and prey animals, he could probably not have multiplied beyond the 10 million mark. But when some 10,000 years ago he began to learn how to cultivate the earth and to domesticate animals, a given land area could supply him with a much greater quantity of food than before. More people born did survive and numbers grew.

As soon as village farming communities began to function, new technologies began to emerge, especially when small food surpluses set villagers free to become artisans specializing in the production and invention of tools. As early as 3000 B.C. the farmers of some Middle East communities had learned to harness draft animals to help them cultivate the soil. This greatly increased man's limited muscle power. From the beginnings of recorded history up to the late Middle Ages, the constant improvement in agricultural techniques facilitated the cultivation of new land and the clearing of forests; hence there were substantial gains in agricultural output, followed by population increases. A tremendous invention of the eighth century was the wheeled plow, while the invention of the horse collar in the tenth century enabled the horse to pull a plow without being choked.

After the Renaissance, technology, discovery, and research "exploded" in the West. Commercial farming developed, yielding increased agricultural surpluses, which allowed more and more people to live in towns and specialize in commerce, industry, and services. The economic base of the population was broadened again, the population ceiling moved up, and numbers grew fast.

Around the middle of the eighteenth century there began in Britain what is commonly called the industrial revolution, which implied a speeding up of the tempo of technological advance and transformation. Britain was followed by other countries, and the frontiers that stemmed population were removed once again, but now in a truly spectacular manner.

As was to be expected, population grew fast, that of the United Kingdom, for example, doubling twice during the nineteenth century. One revolution fed the other. In 1840 a German chemist demonstrated that plant life held mainly three components, namely, potash, phosphorus, and nitrogen—a discovery that subsequently enabled chemists to produce artificial fertilizers. With the construction of railways and steamships a high-capacity and low-cost transport system became available. It enabled millions of Europeans to emigrate to the United States and Canada, and assisted as they were by a massive flow of capital, they opened up and developed the Western Hemisphere. Huge food surpluses were produced by land-rich America, and trains and ships brought them in no time to the Old World. Especially the unprecedented expansion of wheat production on the grasslands of the western United States and Canada eliminated local food shortages there and facilitated the growth of riches in the Western world and the emergence of large cities in northwestern Europe and the Northeast of the United States. More and better food certainly reduced death rates, thus contributing to population growth. Yet by our present-day standards, life expectancy remained short until the twentieth century, even in the rapidly developing Western world.

It was only after the eighteenth century that the impact of scientific medicine and national public health practices on mortality began to be felt.

Mortality in the West

In the past the difference between birth and death rates was usually quite small. There have been periods of population growth during which the death rate was comparatively low; but in numerous cases these "good times" have been followed by periods of war, epidemics, and famine which partly or totally nullified the increase of earlier periods. Hence phases of numerical increase alternated with periods of decimation, sometimes with ages of stability in between.

It was not until the seventeenth and eighteenth centuries that the reduction in the death rate, hence a steady increase in numbers, became a regular phenomenon in the Western world. Presently (1974) the death rate in the more developed countries is 9.2 per thousand.

The bubonic plague of the fourteenth century, for instance, carried over a quarter of Europe's population to the grave. Smallpox was another killer until the discoveries of Edward Jenner (1798) initiated massive vaccination, which has saved millions of lives. Smallpox apparently caused 10 percent of all deaths in eighteenth-century Europe. Since it tended to kill children rather than adults, it was labeled "the poor man's friend," the friend of those poor who happened to be burdened with a large family. Some other well-known scourges were cholera, diphtheria, scarlet fever, typhoid fever, measles, venereal diseases, and tuberculosis.

Most medieval towns were insanitary places. The walls around them impeded the free circulation of air; the dead were often buried within the walls, so that the decayed corpses could by seepage contaminate the town water supply from wells and springs. Garbage, human excreta, and even the offal from slaughterhouses were in some places thrown into the streets, to transform towns into hotbeds of diseases such as typhoid and dysentery.

The early industrial towns of the eighteenth and nineteenth centuries were not much better, perhaps worse. Plumbing and municipal sanitation were nonexistent; accumulated filth seeped into the local wells; garbage was not collected; and in some cities such as London, small streams served certain areas simultaneously as sewers and sources of water supply—a situation that produced what amounted to chronic starvation for part of the population. For obvious reasons, urban death rates were usually higher than their rural counterparts.

With mortality, and especially infant mortality, so high, many of those born never reached maturity, so never reproduced themselves. In addition, infanticide was probably practiced on a wider scale than is usually recognized. It has been estimated that even as late as 1878 about 6 percent of all violent deaths in England were attributable to infanticide. Babies were abandoned in fields and parks or thrown into rivers and canals. They were smothered, strangled, or dosed with gin, or their skulls were smashed. An English newspaper complained in the mid-nineteenth century that infanticide had become a national institution. Yet in 1750 life expectancy had already risen to approximately thirty-five years in the most favored countries of northwest Europe. Considering that life expectancy in earlier periods hardly ever exceeded twenty-five, this was real progress. Around 1850 it had risen to forty years and in 1900 to fifty years.

These improvements were, as stated earlier, due to better supplies of food and other necessities. Periodic famines ceased to occur. Next came public health improvements, consisting of better water supplies and their chlorination, sewage disposal, garbage collection and its sanitary disposal. Housing also improved, and people began to understand the elementary principles of personal hygiene (use of soap, and so on) and disinfection. Cotton began to replace woolen underwear, and the intrinsic nature of many diseases began to be understood through the work of Pasteur, Koch, and others. It should, however, be emphasized that the changes summarized above occurred slowly. In most large American and European cities, safe filtered water, which drastically reduced the incidence of typhoid, only became available around the turn of the present century. The twentieth century also witnessed a medical revolution—accelerated after the1930s—with the discovery of sulfonamides and antibiotics, which permitted effective control of that most important source of death, the whole range of bacterial diseases, especially the ruthless killers pneumonia, typhoid, and diphtheria.

Mortality in the Less Developed Countries

With regard to mortality, the less developed countries have gone through a somewhat different evolution. Perhaps the most important difference between the developed and developing countries is that in the latter the decline in mortality has not coincided with economic expansion.

Many less developed societies have at one stage been colonies, and in many cases, like that of Indonesia, the death rate was reduced by the colonial administration's suppression of wars and quarrels between ethnic groups, and by the introduction of discoveries in the field of hygiene and medicine. The improvement of transport by the construction of a railway network in India by the English, for example, eliminated local famines. Post-1920 discoveries in the fields of public health, hygiene, and scientific medicine were increasingly transplanted to the less developed regions. An acceleration of this evolution took place after 1945, when most of these gained their independence. The low-income countries benefited from the accumulated new developments in the area of death control techniques in the more advanced nations over a long period of time. The transplantation of public health measures and medical care to Asia, Africa, and Latin America has in some cases even been financed by outside sources such as the World Health Organization. The fact is that effective control of bacterial and parasitic diseases can now often be achieved at minimum cost. The usual example cited in relevant population literature is Ceylon, where malaria used to be a major scourge; DDT spraying of all dwellings helped to cut the death rate in half between 1946 and 1954, malaria cases falling from 3 million to less than 40,000, at a cost of under $2 per head, mostly financed from abroad.

In short, mortality is declining rapidly in the less developed regions; hence life expectancy is rising. With the sharp decline in infant and adolescent mortality, more children reach maturity and can propagate their kind; but in many cases the rapid reductions in mortality occurred in the absence of major improvements in living standards. Presently, the average death rate of all less developed countries is 14.3 per thousand. It is estimated to decline to 7.6 per thousand by the turn of the century.

Births in the More Advanced Nations

The nineteenth century witnessed a gradual decline in death rates in the Western world; but in addition, alongside the decline in mortality, birthrates also began to fall, especially in the latter part of the nineteenth century. At present in most advanced countries the birthrates are low, although often still somewhat higher than death rates. This movement from high birth and death rates to controlled low birth and death rates has been labeled the "demographic transition" or the "vital revolution," the reference being to the changeover from a primitive demographic regime with birthrates from 30 to 45 per thousand and death rates from 30 to 40 per thousand, to an advanced one characterized by low mortality and fertility. An essential element in this well-documented theory is the fact that the decline in death rates long outdistances that in birthrates, so that there is an intermediate stage during which birthrates are still high while death rates are steadily declining.

It is at this stage that population grows very fast or even "explodes." Some of the reasons for birthrates' starting to decline were already understood by such nineteenth-century observers as the English economist N. W. Senior and the French social scientist Arsène Dumont, who argued that as prosperity rises above a certain threshold, a taste for more comfort and convenience develops, as well as a feeling of degradation in their absence. Moreover, the gradual democratization of society, with approximately equal rights and opportunities but unequal incomes, tends to enhance competition. Hence men began to postpone their marriages and limit their families in order to promote their chances of social and economic advance. Kipling once said, "From the utmost tropics up to the pole, he travels fastest who travels alone." In a democratic urban environment a large family is an obstacle to the career-oriented citizen.

In explanation of declining birthrates in the West, modern population literature usually points to the following determinants:

1. Spread of literacy and improved formal schooling;
2. The rising cost of rearing and educating children in a modern urban environment;
3. The emancipation of women and their increasing employment in gainful occupations outside the home;
4. A decline in religious interest;
5. More rational attitudes and modes of thinking;
6. Greater availability of contraceptive knowledge and effective contraceptives.

Births in the Low-Income Areas

We noted that the transplantation of public health facilities and improved medical care from the West to the developing countries can reduce the death rate quickly and at relatively little cost. In the West the decline in birthrates arose endogenously with economic progress and profound changes in the political and social framework. In developing countries in general, reductions in mortality have been accompanied by little change in fertility levels; in most there has been little economic progress, and the transition from a traditional to a modern society has been in many cases painfully slow if it has occurred at all. Hence birthrates in developing countries remained very high and tended, if anything, to rise slightly because in some of these countries the quantity and quality of available food supplies showed a mild increase. The improved health conditions enable more females to survive throughout their entire reproductive period, thus enhancing the power to multiply of the populations to which they belong. It has been said that, if these nations would continue to combine prehistoric birthrates with twentieth-century death rates, they would ultimately collapse under the weight of numbers, just as apple trees can collapse under the weight of their overloaded branches. Hardly any low-income country has presently reached the relatively low level of fertility which northwestern Europe had attained a century ago.

What Lies Ahead

Prospects are that more population increase still lies in the future. The following five demographic situations are to be distinguished in clarification of that point:

1. Birthrates and death rates are both high and virtually cancel each other out. Such a situation typically prevailed in traditional agricultural societies.
2. The death rate is falling because of improvements in public health measures and medicine, the birthrate remaining high.
3. The death rate has fallen substantially and continues to decline; now the birthrate also begins to decline. However, mortality is well below fertility, so population rapidly increases.

4. Both birth and death rates are low, but death rates are still lower than birthrates. Fluctuations are wider in the birthrate than in the death rate.
5. Birth and death rates are low and equal, population growth is nil.

The economically advanced nations of the West and Japan are in stage 4 or 5. Most countries in the world, containing at least two-thirds of the planet's population, have just started the demographic transition and are either in phase 2 or 3, in which most demographic growth occurs. As a result the populations of the less developed countries will grow fast; from about 2.5 billion in 1970 to about 5 billion in the year 2000. The populations of the more developed countries are expected to grow from 1.090 million in 1970 to 1.454 million at the end of our century.

In Western Europe and North America the transition from high birth and death rates to low ones was induced by a basic modernization process. The trajectory was painfully long. It took England and Wales about seventy years to proceed from stage 1 of the demographic transition to stage 4.

There is, however, some evidence that a number of countries that started the transition at a later date than the Western nations completed it at a faster rate. Southern European countries such as Italy, central European nations such as Poland, and one Asian country (that is, Japan) have achieved a faster reduction in their fertility levels than the early starters. There is therefore some hope (but no certainty) that the less developed countries, which are nearly all experiencing some measure of social and economic progress, will witness an accelerated transition. Certain specific developing areas such as Taiwan, South Korea, Hong Kong, Singapore, and Puerto Rico are in fact undergoing an acceleration in their process of fertility decline. These areas, however, are small, while a discernible rise in per capita incomes is materializing. Other social indicators such as literacy levels and measures of health and nutrition also show that major changes are under way. Yet there remain a substantial number of very large countries such as India, Western Pakistan, Indonesia, and Nigeria that do not seem to be moving.

2

Why people have children

Children's children are the glory of old men, and the glory of children are their father's.

Proverbs 17:6

An Ill-Explored Area

We noted in the previous chapter that the present population explosion is due to the worldwide decline in death rates. Especially in the less developed countries, this decline in mortality has not been followed by a decline in fertility—which brings us to the question: Why do people have as many (or as few) children as they have? In the more developed countries the decline in fertility has not been persistent. During the 1930s, for instance, fertility was low in most countries of the Western world. After 1944 it rose again; people began to have somewhat larger families. Since 1957 fertility in the West has been gradually dropping once more. Such questions as why the poor usually have larger families than the rich are also relevant. It would, after all, be reasonable to expect those who can afford more children to have more; but statistical evidence does not support this assumption.

It should be said at the outset that the reasons why people want their families to be of a certain size are not yet adequately understood, nor has much research been done in this area. Much knowledge about the factors that affect sexual and reproductive behavior still consists of hypotheses awaiting further testing.

Fertility research also seems to suggest that the notion that a birth is either wanted or unwanted is too simplistic. All surveys show that there is a large area of indifference.

No effort will be made here to work out a consistent conceptual framework for fertility analysis. A brief catalogue of some of the perceived financial and psychic benefits parents derive from children as compared with the perceived financial and psychic costs is all that will be attempted.

Yet such a list will, it is hoped, help create a deeper understanding of reproductive behavior. A review of some attitudinal factors inhibiting birth control is also in order, as well as a discussion of why people accept children passively.

Throughout our investigation we shall assume that individual fertility behavior reflects the best accommodation of individual drives and desires to the impositions of the environment. People make choices, the essential characteristic of the process being that one course of action is traded off against another. Although perhaps not entirely satisfactory, this framework is probably the most practical available.

There follows a list of reasons why people desire children.

Economic Benefits of Children

It may be true that in the more developed countries children yield little or no economic benefit. In many of the less developed countries, however, children do have economic value, so that reproduction can sometimes be a rewarding activity. First, they often help on the farm or in the family business while growing up. Young boys and girls can assist adults in sowing seed. Boys especially can help the men at harvest time, while girls can help the women to carry the grain home. Young boys can also watch over cattle and take them to pasture. Girls can help their mothers in the preparation and cooking of food from the age of six onward, besides doing other household chores. At the age of seven or so, they begin to take care of younger children.

Children may also work for small wages that are turned over to their parents. Grown-up sons may continue to share their earnings with the parents. In peasant societies, therefore, children often become productive after a comparatively short investment period. With economic development the child becomes less of an economic asset because schooling time is lengthened; when this is the case and child labor is legislated out of existence, the productive utility of the child falls sharply.

Another economic reason why children may be desired is that parents, especially those who have had no opportunity to save and invest, rely on them for security in old age, particularly in traditional societies, where loyalty to the parents tends to be high. If the amount of help to be expected in old age depends on the number of children alive in the adults' declining years, it is wise to have at least several children in case some die.

In the more developed countries, a minimal amount of security in old age is usually provided through collective private or governmental programs. Hence children need no longer be valued as a source of old age insurance. As areas become urbanized and industrialized, children tend to move away from the parents' village. There is also greater uncertainty as to whether employment can be found. Moreover, as societies develop, the family becomes more nuclear and ties with the parents tend to weaken. Support may not come forth when needed. Hence people become less willing to undergo the hardship of a large family as the prospects for security in old age become more dubious.

Biological Benefits of Children: Children Satisfy Innate Needs for Motherhood

Although "innate needs for motherhood" are hard to define, there is the notion of woman's desire to carry a baby, to go through delivery and childbirth, and to care for and protect an infant.

Psychic Benefits of Children: The Give-and-Take of Affection

One reason for wanting children is the need for someone to love plus the need to be loved. Children also provide companionship and opportunity for interaction and play. There is some evidence that those who want small families are more motivated by love of children than those who want large families, the latter type of parents seeming more motivated by specific gains, such as a sense of power and of accomplishment. It has been argued that modern society makes relationships more impersonal and thus reduces the number of relation-

ships in which one can express warmth and affection. The presence of
children permits such expression and eliminates loneliness.

Researchers have noted that, particularly in the lower-income
classes, children compensate for that lack of affectionate response
wives sometimes find in their husbands, children even becoming the
woman's chief source of affection.

Children as the True Admission Ticket to Adulthood

Parenthood establishes adulthood in a society, where a person who
becomes father or mother is thereby considered truly mature, stable,
and accepted. This fact seems truer for women than for men.
Especially for the lower-class woman who has few interests, motherhood is often regarded as what life is all about. By having children,
women become respectable and worthwhile. Young women (perhaps
decreasingly so in the United States) may feel somewhat uncertain
about their role and importance in society. Having a child accords
them a role and gives their lives a meaning. Worthwhile employment
openings compete with this, and as more and more careers become
open to women, the importance of offspring is somewhat lessened.

Children as Virility Symbols

Children are sometimes desired to demonstrate one's sexual adequacy to the outside world. Sexual potency is not clearly visible; children
are! Moreover, the man who becomes a father proves he is able, not only
to have orgasms, but also to impregnate. The wife may also be happy
at the assurance that she is not sterile. For a young man in certain
rural areas of Indonesia, the birth of his first child means the full recognition of adulthood. He is entitled to different attentions and is expected to bear different responsibilities. In Puerto Rico men usually
want a first child immediately after marriage, because a child, especially a son, is the socially accepted indication of true manliness. A childless married man or a producer only of girls is an object of rediculc
and pity. It might possibly be speculated that, the greater the man's uncertainty and anxiety about his virility, the greater his emotional need
to assert it. The desire for a rapid succession of births may, at least in
some societies, betray the need for repeated proof of potency.

It has also been argued that in the context of such societies as Puerto Rico, or even the United States, frustration in the economic sphere may lead to a desire for additional conceptions. For many a lower-class man, all avenues to prestige seem blocked, as he has neither the capital nor the education to climb up the social ladder; but if one can have a large family and support it, one has still given proof of one's masculinity and one's capacity to do things—which enhances self-esteem.

It goes without saying that ascetic religions like Catholicism, with their traditional emphasis on abstinence, continence, and virginity, may well help to create deep inner doubts about sexual adequacy and set up compensatory mechanisms in some individuals. Where a particular religion regards sexual gratification as a source of impurity and sin, individuals brought up in it may live in a state of quasi-permanent insecurity, if not panic, about their sexual adequacy. The sole logical consequence would be a compulsive urge to prove one's potency to oneself and others. This may perhaps explain the obsessive preoccupation of so many Latin American males with their *machismo*.

Children as an Extension of the Self

Children are often seen as an extension of oneself, and in that sense provide a form of narcissistic gratification. But many spouses also feel the need to "extrapolate" themselves beyond their own lifetimes. Having children connects one up with the future; something of oneself lives on, so to speak, to bring one closer to immortality. Think, too, in this context of the joy of transmitting one's cultural heritage and learning to one's children.

Power

Within the small, as well as the extended, family the woman gains some power as soon as she becomes a mother. Parents also have more power and influence over a child than they are ever likely to have over any other living person. For some people, especially those who hardly ever get a chance to influence others through social status, this may be most gratifying.

Achievement

Parents may derive satisfaction not only from the physical production of the child but from meeting the challenges that the rearing of the child necessarily involves. To bring up a healthy and productive child provides an outlet for creativity and demonstrates capability.

Family Name

Some people keep having children until they have at least one boy who continues the family name. Recent research has shown that husbands emphasize this aspect more than their wives.

Fear of Repudiation

Observers of countries where Islam is the dominant religion have noted that women sometimes desire large families because they believe that it reduces their chances of being abandoned. As is known, Islam allows men to repudiate their wives with only very minimal formalities. A large family presumably ties the husband to the family.

Entertainment

Children provide fun and entertainment; one can play games with them and legitimately reassume childhood roles. A new child provides a new experience. The element of novelty is paramount.

Social Influences Stimulating the Desire for Children

The demands, pressures, and impositions of his environment shape man's preferences, outlook, and needs.

If, for instance, in a peasant society barrenness in the female is a disgrace, she is strongly motivated toward pregnancy. In several of the more traditional peasant societies the barren woman is scorned, pitied, and sometimes ostracized. Parents and friends may also exercise pressure on couples. The influence of certain pronatalist religions, like Roman Catholicism, is well known. In North America as well as in Latin America there exists a positive relationship between commitment to church doctrine and fertility.

Economic Costs of Children

The first costs involved in the raising of children are the "direct" or "cash" costs. Children must be fed, clothed, sheltered. They attend school and need medical care. Occasional extras must be provided, and after a certain age pocket money must be supplied. All such costs can be measured in dollars or other currency units. As soon as legislation does away with child labor and makes education compulsory, the costs of raising children go up, especially for the lower-income groups. Migration from country to town also tends to raise the direct costs of children. It is usually cheaper to bring up children on a farm or village.

Economists like Gary Becker have made a useful distinction between "direct costs" of children and "expenditures" on children. The costs of a given-quality child are the same for all social classes in any population, being determined by the market prices of the basket goods and services the child consumes during rearing. Parents are, of course, free to change the makeup of the "basket," that is, to modify expenditures on a given child, and so to change the child's "quality." The child may be given expensive foods and high-quality clothing, may be sent to private schools, and so on. Sociologists like Judith Blake have pointed to the strong social pressures on wealthier parents to increase the amounts they spend on their children. When parents are prosperous, they must supply their children with high-quality food, shelter, clothing, and education, all part of the life-style at their social level. And to give their offspring the competitive advantages of their class, they send them to expensive private schools and universities. The parents believe, in fact, that such expenditures cannot really be avoided—which may partially explain why the higher-income groups tend to have low fertility levels.

Opportunity Costs

When economists speak of "opportunity costs," they mean the value of foregone opportunities or of sacrifices made to obtain something—in this case an additional child. Opportunity costs here are of three kinds. First, parents must sacrifice certain consumption expenditures if the costs of an additional child are to be met. Second, additional children make saving for old age more difficult. Again, the smaller the family in a peasant society, the more funds are available for improvements on the farm, given a certain income. A third opportunity cost consists of the earnings the wife must forego. The more children there are in a family, the more the wife is confined to the home. When the wife is highly skilled, the foregone earnings may be substantial, especially when employment opportunities are abundant.

In a traditional peasant society the opportunity costs of additional children may not be too high, as the wife can supervise the children while still working on the family farm. In the first stages of economic development, work opportunities seem to dwindle; but later, when prospects of education and female employment open up, the opportunity costs of extra children apparently rise sharply.

Psychic Costs

The fact that children tie the mother to the home implies a psychic cost. Each child increases the amount of housework to be done. Outside interests and activities, as well as contacts with other adults, have to be reduced. Especially for the educated middle-class woman, this amounts to at least some degree of intellectual impoverishment.

In this context it may also be mentioned that the higher-income groups tend to be the most engrossed in the evolution of their offspring; so these groups spend much personal attention on their children, who therefore sharply compete for time and effort. As these same people tend to be highly involved in their careers, their tendency to have children is usually less than that of the lower-income groups.

Housekeeping Tasks

The more children there are, the more meals have to be cooked and the more clothes to be washed. Children are messy, and more housecleaning becomes necessary. Needless to say, the housekeeping tasks affect different women differently; some may actually like them. Another problem is that the housework goes on whether mother's health is good or not.

Health

Constant childbearing tends to wreck the mother's health. Even a few children may affect the health of a mother. In addition, the drudgery that children impose on the mother may also weaken her resistance and physical condition. Mothers of large families are often less robust than those of small families. Again, children, especially young ones, may cause loss of sleep and rest by needing attention during the night.

Intimacy and Privacy

When children arrive, communication and romance within the marriage often diminish. The spouses converse less with each other and have less time and opportunity to do things together. With children around there is less privacy and chance for intimacy; not only do the spouses tend to devote less time and attention to each other; but in addition, each individual child gets less affection and care as the family grows. It may be observed here that relevant studies indicate a negative influence of large sibship size on children's performance in school, with verbal abilities and reading skills most affected. Such results suggest a less intensive interaction with adults by children from large families.

It Is Not Just the Demand for Children That Counts

Until now we have considered merely the number of children parents wish to have. It would be naive to believe that this factor alone determines "completed fertility," that is, the number of children a couple will have produced during their reproductive, fertile period. Couples want, not only so many children, but also something else, namely, sexual gratification, whether or not it results in pregnancy. Contraception can safeguard a couple from this uncertainty; but it has its own costs, financial and psychic. Therefore the couple not only weighs the advantages against the inconveniences of another child, but also balances the psychic and cash costs of contraception against the benefits of protection against conception.

For many people the emotional and pecuniary costs of contraception are considerable. In order to plan a family properly, the spouses must discuss the desired family size. Contraceptive information must be sought; the woman often has to visit a physician. Contraceptive devices having to be obtained from him, from the family planning clinic, or from the drugstore, all such approaches are likely to imply high psychic costs for some people. People wishing to plan their family must be future-oriented. The idea of discussing contraception and sexual matters together is still painful, if not repellent, to many married people.

Gaining a better understanding of the male and female anatomy, as of the basic facts of sex and contraception, can arouse tensions and anxiety. Numerous women find it utterly embarrassing to be examined by a male physician. Many husbands cannot accept it either because they don't want their wife's body to be examined by "another man."

The use of contraception may clash with religious beliefs. Women are sometimes afraid to be seen in birth control clinics for fear of other people knowing that they are interested in contraception. Both men and women are sometimes too shy to ask for contraceptives in a drugstore. There are, lastly, many popular superstitions about contraceptives, usually based on ignorance of the male and female anatomy. Some people believe that condoms and jellies can cause diseases like cancer or tuberculosis. There is a fear that intrauterine devices (IUDs) and diaphragms can move into other organs such as the bladder or the lungs. The birth control pill raises fears of being unsexed, poisoned, or physically damaged. Condoms especially are said to diminish sexual pleasure. Foam tablets, condoms, and jellies are said to be messy. The whole question of sterilization is also anxiety-laden, as it is sometimes believed to cause impotence or decreased vigor in the male or disease in the female. In some cultures the men fear that sterilization or even use of the IUD will encourage promiscuity in "their" women. The greater the mutual suspicion between the sexes, the likelier this is to happen.

This category of psychic costs in particular apparently induces many couples to ignore the whole issue and to fall back on a passive type of behavior. Especially among the lower-income classes, where training in coping with general problems is likely to be the poorest, rejection of an active and constructive attitude and submission to whatever "fate" may bring are often the commoner attitudes. The alternative of passive resignation is preferred, and when "unwanted" children are born, fate or providence is blamed. The world as some lower-income persons see it is chaotic and confusing; they can hardly think of themselves as controlling what happens in their lives. Wife-husband communication is often poor, and the unwillingness of either spouse or both to worry about the future manifests itself in an exclusive escape type of preoccupation with the small pleasures and problems of the moment.

For some couples the cash costs of contraception are still considerable, although rising incomes and/or family planning programs are a great help in providing them with cheap or free relief. In the United States, fertility has declined again since 1957, perhaps partly because rising incomes have made contraception relatively cheaper. More favorable attitudes toward contraception, the reversal of long-accepted puritanical customs, wider public discussion of contraception, and relaxation and modernization of laws dealing with birth control have all substantially reduced the psychic costs of contraception.

How It All Works Out

Our basic argumention in this chapter is that what couples will or will not actually do reflects what they believe to be the best available compromise between (1) their basic, possibly conflicting, needs, inclinations, impulses, and desires, and (2) the environment, or the social conditions under which they live. In other words, couples contemplating another child will, within the framework of their income and preferences, balance the advantages of an added child against the inconveniences, while at the same time weighing the cost against the benefits of contraception. The impositions of the environment are also considered. People will go on having children as long as the perceived advantages exceed the inconveniences and will stop when the cost and benefits of the last child born just equate, because from then on the inconveniences will be greater than the benefits. Any couple hesitating between taking the risk of having another child and making the effort of contraception will balance advantages against costs. Should they finally decide not to bother with contraception, it is because they regard the perceived inconveniences of another possible addition to the family as less than the subjective and/or financial costs of practicing birth control. It is a good question whether the weighing of benefits against costs is always at the conscious level. At all events, the outcome of the decision does in a way reflect the maximization of satisfaction or the minimization of hardship and discomfort, in the sense that any other decision than the one taken would create less benefit or more discomfort.

Wanted children are the result of a positive decision to have another child by a couple possibly willing to practice contraception should they not wish to have more children. Often enough, however, conception occurs on account of a negative decision not to prevent pregnancy because it is too bothersome to try. The children thus produced, although possibly accepted, are not truly "wanted" children.

Societal facilitators like customs favoring childbearing and societal barriers like norms discouraging it do have their influence on the perceived costs and benefits as well. Unfortunately, in many low-income countries societal factors encourage rather than discourage childbearing.

In countries where family-planning services are either not available or too expensive for the majority of the population, the options available to a couple are severely limited. The choice between abstention or constant childbearing implies great hardship, and in countries where this is the only alternative many, most, couples will perhaps tend to prefer the hardship large families imply. Population is likely to grow fast; so the introduction of widespread cheap family-planning services is not only a great humanitarian measure, but also one likely to contribute substantially to the reduction of population growth rate, although this alone is far from sufficient, as we shall see later.

3

The population boosters

> *Acquisitiveness, vanity, rivalry and love of power are, after the basic instincts, the prime movers of all that happens in politics.*
>
> Bertrand Russell

Foxes and Rabbits

In the previous chapter an attempt was made to give some idea of the various attitudes motivating individual decisions as to childbearing. In many countries there are groups, creeds, and institutions that endeavor to influence this personal decision-making process by exercising a variety of pronatalist pressures on the individual that sometimes take the form of contraception baiting. Examination of these population pushers and their special interests leads to the suspicion that it is usually the foxes that advise the rabbits to have large families. Although they may be in fact mistaken, these pronatalist pressure groups tend to believe that they have something to gain from population expansion.

The Roman Catholic Church

Although there are many church liberals who believe that the time has come for the Catholic church to end its opposition to artificial birth control, the conservative view still dominates the teachings of

the church; in 1968 Papal Encyclical *Humanae Vitae* forbade artificial contraception and permitted married couples only the use of the
rhythm method.

American Catholics have not responded positively to *Humanae
Vitae*. In fact, during the 1960s and 1970s Catholic couples have increasingly adopted birth control methods other than the rhythm
method. Between 1965 and 1970 the percentage of Catholic women
not acting in keeping with the teachings of the church on birth control
rose from 50 percent to 69 percent. The increase in noncompliance
among very young married Catholic women is particularly striking.
According to the fertility studies of Charles F. Westoff, among women
aged twenty to twenty-four the proportion not following the rules on
contraception laid down by the church rose from 30 percent in 1955 to
78 percent by 1970.

Natural Law

Some Catholic writers and church authorities, among them Pope
Pius XI, have based their opposition to contraception on the argument that it is unnatural to interfere with the physiological consequences of the sexual act. The difficult question arises: What is
natural? It certainly seems a long time since man still behaved
"naturally," in the sense of leaving nature's processes alone. Even
organized agriculture, which is believed to have started some 8,000
years ago, is unnatural. Living "naturally" would imply really a
return to primitive nudity and to a hunting and food-gathering
existence; but living in organized communities with governmental
and administrative institutions is certainly a far cry from living
"naturally." And, were we to live a "natural" life, we should certainly
abstain from cooked food, soap, umbrellas, heated or air-conditioned
dwellings, cars, planes, hospitals, and some thousands of other items.
All public health programs would be abolished, since death control is
also "unnatural." Is marriage itself natural? Probably not! There is
little reason to believe that "natural man" awaited the sanction of a
priest to mate.

Increase and Multiply

Many Catholic writers and authorities refer to the existence of
"revealed supernatural truths" such as "be fruitful and multiply and

replenish the earth," a text twice repeated in the book of Genesis. Although this commandment is used as an argument against any limitation of the number of births, the text, examined carefully, contains its own limitation. Those commanded were told to "replenish the earth." Although man has not had much success in obeying other biblical commandments, such as "Thou shall not kill," he has in this particular instance been triumphant. With 4 billion inhabitants the world can now be considered to be fully "replenished." The historical context of the injunction also merits some consideration; that is, the commandment was first given to a solitary pair living in an empty world but was later repeated to the eight survivors (Noah and his family) of a deluge that had destroyed all other life on earth.

Another awkward question is the Catholic church's insistence on celibacy for priests and nuns, which might be seen as a straight defiance of the command to be fruitful and multiply.

Moral Decadence

Such an esteemed author as Father De Lestapis (*Family Planning and Modern Problems*) believes that generalized contraception will lead to nothing less than the degradation of family life, immaturity of spouses, eroticism, and homosexuality. A Costa Rican priest wrote in *La Republica* (August 8, 1968) that family and society were menaced by unbraked sensualism and hedonism; but the Encyclical *Humanae Vitae*, he concluded, had saved the world from moral ruin. Traditionally, the Catholic church has had a high moral and religious attitude to virginity and sexual continence. Sexual intercourse was regarded as a moral lapse. However, since mating and procreation are inexorably related, intercourse is permitted in marriage if the spouses want another child. Contraception does two things: (1) By disconnecting mating and impregnation, it suggests that sexual intercourse can be indulged in at any time for recreation as well as procreation, and (2) reliable contraceptives abolish the fear of pregnancy, the undoubted powerful deterrent to sexual relations and, therefore, deprive the traditional virginity-oriented ethical code of one of its main supports. No wonder that generalized contraception looks threatening to some champions of conventional morality!

The Weight of History

A major point in our world view is the fact that what is "age-old" is endowed with a particular sanctity. Christian morality was born in a fertility-worshiping environment. Many different peoples around the Mediterranean, at the time Christianity emerged and spread, adored gods and goddesses such as Isis and Astarte representing the reproductive, life-giving principle. This generative power was recognized in men, animals, and the soil and was believed to be of divine origin. In those times of rudely organized societies man's well-being and safety were very closely related to fertility and reproduction because they ensured abundant crops, the multiplication of his cattle, the supply of young males to defend the community in times of danger, and the availability of sons and daughters to help on the farm and in the house. Everything seemed to depend on this vital and sacred power to create life. Phallic worship was the basis of many festivals and religious ceremonies. As the areas around the Mediterranean became increasingly urbanized and skepticism grew, the "pure" agricultural origins of fertility worship were progressively forgotten, while the licentious aspects were anxiously preserved; but here the emphasis of so many Christian writers on the worst features of pagan civilization is probably exaggerated. Yet the early Christians operated in an ethically worn-out environment, their opposition to which took them to the other extreme: declaration of war on sex. Saint Paul clearly identified the flesh with evil ("mortify your members which are upon the earth," "flee fornication," etc.). Paul mortified his body and submitted himself to fasting, cold, nakedness, and vigils. Worldly renunciation, asceticism, and sexual abstinence became common among the early Christians. Many went to wild extremes; Origen emasculated himself in youth; Athanasius never washed his feet; certain hermits lived in dried-out wells or tombs, or spent long weeks in the depths of thorn bushes. A new sexual code emerged; licentiousness was sinful, virginity and abstinence glorious, and marriage at best pardonable.

The new sexual morality was crystallized in the works of Saint Augustine, whose work on "The Good of Marriage" remains a cornerstone of present-day Christian doctrine on sex and procreation. While young, this father of the church had participated in the unbridled licentiousness of his homeland, North Africa. In "The

Good of Marriage" he states, however, that marriage is no more than tolerated. Procreation is its only justification, the one reason for its acceptance, although continence and virginity are under all circumstances to be preferred, and anything beyond the need for generation is sinful and defiling.

Sixteen centuries separate us from Saint Augustine; but the church's attitude is still marked by the past. Such is the weight of tradition!

At the same time, however, the church heaps praise on prolific parents, calls procreation a holy function, and claims that family size should be left in God's hands. In that sense the church has returned to a thinly disguised variety of the fertility worship that characterized the pagan religions which preceded Christianity and which the early Christians opposed. As stated earlier, the very essence of phallicism (fertility worship) was precisely that reverence, as well as worship, was paid to the reproductive or generative powers.

The Nationalists

Nationalism, which some have defined as "feelings of loyalty and devotion to one's nation," has often turned into chauvinistic or integral nationalism, the type characterized by an excessive craving for prestige and power for one's own nation, and whenever power and prestige are associated with greater numbers, chauvinistic nationalism often tends to turn natalist. Between 1450 and 1750, European countries adopted a nationalistic politico-economic philosophy, usually known as "mercantilism," which was associated with the rise of tough, grasping national states intent on increasing their power and enlarging their territories. For various reasons, among them "power," writers and statesmen of this period favored large and growing populations. Mercantilism was dead by 1800; but the last quarter of the nineteenth century witnessed a new outbreak of exaggerated national self-consciousness. Nationalism plus imperialism sought population growth to ease the nation's "need" for power and prestige and to supply the human resources for ambitious colonization programs.

France's defeat in 1870 by Germany fostered nationalistic sentiments born of the fear that France's population would be too small to win in another war. Germany's population, in fact, increased faster than that of France. Here we have the beginnings of a nationalistic pronatalist tradition linked with an urge toward national "grandeur" that is still with us.

Germany and Italy, now unified, had also their share of nationalistic chauvinism. They envied the British and French their relatively large colonial empires, and some of their writers and politicians argued that their respective countries needed to conquer new territories, too, in order to have outlets for "excess population." At the same time they favored population growth in their own countries (though not in others), because this to them was a sign of vitality, health, and national virility. Chauvinistic nationalism finally led to World War I, and ultimately to World War II.

In matters of population the fascist and National Socialist writers and statesmen eagerly built on the nationalistic arguments of the writers of the last quarter of the nineteenth century. They complained about demographic maladjustment, population pressure, and lack of space in their countries and the need for colonies and new territories to accommodate surplus numbers, at the same time doing all in their power to increase demographic congestion. The National Socialist and fascist press engaged in heavy pronatalist propaganda; family allowances were given to prolific parents, plus tax rebates, and birth control was suppressed.

In the 1930s Japan joined Italy and Germany as a "dissatisfied power" and began to sing the same song. She attempted to stimulate population by the same methods, complained simultaneously about population pressure, and proclaimed the need for an empire. Any suggestion by spokesmen of other European nations or the United States that population pressure might be eased by birth control measures was explained as just another proof of an evil, widespread conspiracy of these nations against the peoples of Italy, Germany, and Japan. The well-known Italian demographer C. Gini, wrote literally that the satisfied powers (those with colonies) wanted to reduce Italian men to masturbation and castration by denying Italy the "right" to acquire new colonies and fill them with Italians.

Despite the present unprecedented population growth, demographic nationalism is widespread. In France it is still very strong, finding expression in numerous natalist measures to foster population growth such as high family allowances. Many French demographers stress the desirability of expanding population. The statements of nationalistic writers and politicians are usually

stronger. M. Debré, an influential Gaullist politician, argues in his
books (*Au service de la Nation* and *Jeunesse, quelle France te faut-il?*)
that France is underpopulated and that a greater population will
confer prosperity, power, and influence on the country. All this
without much explanation.

In Latin America one finds nationalist pronatalism in the writings of such authors as F. C. Alegre (Peru), H. Vergara (Colombia),
and N. P. Altamirano (El Salvador), who argue that the population
problem, which is usually discussed in terms of comparative density, does not exist in Latin America. South America is an "empty
continent," they say, and population must grow. Growth automatically brings (how? we may ask) much-needed structural change,
civilization, and progress. Recommendations by foreigners or international agencies to reduce fertility and the subsidizing of birth-
control programs prove for these writers the existence of a plot to
keep Latin America weak and undeveloped. The United States is
planning genocide for the Latin American peoples, these writers say.
Castration of all Latin American males is what birth controllers are
after. Birth control is death; the idea is to transform the vigorous
wombs of Latin American mothers into abattoirs. To stop population
is to stop nature. What they (the nationalist writers) stand for is "life,"
etc., etc.

Interestingly, almost identical phrases can be found in the writings
of the nineteenth-century French and German nationalists, later
expanded and developed by fascists and National Socialists.

If, however, the United States or the Western world in general
really wanted to keep low-income areas such as South America weak
and undeveloped, then they should be *discouraging* family planning
and *encouraging* population growth in these regions.

Psychologically oriented writers argue that, although virility and
fertility are two different things at the lower, subconscious level, individuals often equate them. Therefore the idea of fertility reduction
sometimes provokes an obscure fear of emasculation, especially in individuals who are sexually not too well balanced.

Concluding the discussion of nationalism, the present writer does
not think nationalism inherently bad. Many dependent and exploited
nations found perhaps in nationalism the ideological stimulus needed
to free themselves and increase their own self-respect; but history has
shown time and again that nationalism easily becomes proud, intol-

erant, and hostile. The embittered effusions of chauvinistic nationalists are not conducive to peaceful cooperation and mutual respect in
international relations.

Racial Chauvinism

The same craving for power, domination, and more influence that
seems to characterize some nationalists can sometimes be found in
representatives of certain militant racial minority groups who also
equate numbers with power. The well-known Black Muslim leader
Elyah Muhammad urged American blacks not to practice contraception but to be fruitful and multiply. Representatives of the National Association for the Advancement of Colored People have been
known to state that black women should produce more babies until
the blacks constitute about 30 to 35 percent of the population; for
only then, they say, will the blacks be able to impinge on the power
structure of the country. About the suffering large families might
bring to black women and children not a word is said.

Radical Socialism

At this moment there is a wide divergence of views among socialist writers. Where they are "evolutionary," most socialists seem to
favor family planning and accept the usefulness of national birth
control programs. Among "revolutionary" socialists there is more
disagreement. The old Marxist socialists opposed the idea that
poverty and indigency could be caused by fast population growth
and/or high population density, holding that the faulty organization
of society and unequal distribution of income within it were the main
causes of distress. Unemployment, said Marx, confusing overpopulation with unemployment, is caused not by excessive procreation but
by the machine replacing the worker. Automation displaces the
laborer, and mechanization dispenses with muscle power in the
factory. Then women and children can attend machines, too; hence
employers prefer them to male laborers, who cost more in wages.

Marx's friend and disciple Engels, while basically at one with
Marx, nevertheless accepted towards the end of his career the abstract
"possibility" of overpopulation in a Communist society. An Italian
follower of Marx, the theorist Achille Loria, believed that population

growth creates a growing disequilibrium between food production and food requirements; the tension finally becomes so great that the existing economic system collapses and gives way to a superior, more productive one. Loria was apparently thinking of a basically agricultural society like his contemporary Italy. The faster the growth of population, the quicker the transition from less productive to more efficient society. A stable population would put an end to the evolutionary process; but, said Loria (who wrote at the turn of the twentieth century), population continues its upsurge; so at some time in the distant future the capitalist mode of production will be swept away, to be replaced by collective ownership of the land, which Loria thought to be the most productive arrangement in existence.

Like many other Marxist writers, Loria really believed in a single formula, one easy model, to explain the sweep of events; but few prudent scientists would agree that only one or two factors determine history's course.

Lenin wrote that, although population growth creates the need to grow more food on a given area of land, thus perhaps reducing output per man or increasing the cost per unit of food produced, this trend is adequately offset by technical advances and better skills. He rejected reduction of population growth for economic reasons but favored liberalization of such laws on contraception and abortion as existed in Europe around 1900, which, he said, were hypocritical.

Until Stalin's death some Soviet Russian writers, politicians, and delegates at international conferences condemned the idea that population growth or density could jeopardize economic and social progress, qualifying it as fascist, racist, barbarous, cannibalistic, or an attempt at genocide. Soviet Union delegates at United Nations conferences and the Soviet newspaper *Pravda* said in the 1950s that birth control was a "Hitlerite" device used by American warmongers and imperialists set on the extermination of millions of people. Even Khrushchev called birth control a "cannibalistic theory."

Increases in population, it was further argued, could always be accommodated provided the social regime was "right" (i.e., Communist). During the last decade an important evolution has taken place, however, so that several USSR scientists now recognize the heavy burdens fast population growth can place on a nation's socioeconomic development. A number of revolutionary socialists in Africa and Latin America nevertheless still maintain that family

planning is a device used by what they label as "capitalist" and im-
perialist" countries to keep the less developed regions in subjection.
    Some Latin American radical socialists occasionally adopt an in-
tellectual position close to Loria's, arguing that population growth
will lead to the collapse of the "bourgeois" *latifundista* regime, whose
main characteristic is a very uneven distribution of landed property.
Family-planning ideas and programs, they say, are aimed at
stemming population without modifying outworn social structures.
Another of their arguments (by no means the least important) is that
population growth will create masses of unemployed and dissatisfied
young people committed to the destruction of the existing political
and economic framework and the erection of a new Marxist society.

Business

    Business leaders are sometimes known to argue that population
growth is desirable because it supplies good markets for their
products. More people means more customers, hence a greater demand for goods and services, more gross receipts, and possibly more
profits. Population growth does more than merely enlarge markets,
however. It may also lead to the establishment of more rival firms. At
the same time, increased numbers may be at the expense of higher per
capita incomes, a theme that will be developed later in this work.
More people, therefore, often implies that people have less to spend.
The wiser businessmen are increasingly aware of the fact that rising
incomes per person may well provide a better guarantee for expanding markets than just growing numbers.
    Population growth has also been said to provide business firms with
abundant and cheap labor. Given ample labor, the workers'
bargaining power weakens, so that wages may be prevented from
increasing or may even decline. True as this may be, poor workers are
poor clients too, a fact with which the business community itself is
familiar.

Conclusion

    The supporters of pronatalist programs and ideas often assume
that these will somehow enhance the adoption of the kind of societal
structures they prefer or will promote the special interests of their own

group or class, conceiving of the common man as a tool for the promotion of their own particular advantage, but apparently they are little concerned with the effects of population on community or individual welfare.

4

Population and political stability

We have no choice except as between evils.
Joseph A. Schumpeter

Sharp Rise in the Number of Adolescents and Young Adults

Over the next thirty to forty years, world population is certain to increase by leaps and bounds. The absolute number of young people in the world will rise steeply. In many less developed countries the proportion of young people will also increase.

The decline in mortality due to health improvements experienced by the less developed countries over several decades tends to accrue to infants and small children rather than to the old. Ameliorations in health and medicine typically reduce infant mortality most dramatically; more children survive to mature ages. Once they enter the reproductive period, they serve to raise the number of births. Infant mortality, now down to about 20 per thousand births or less in the healthier countries, was commonly at least ten times more under more primitive conditions. Before 1940 there were still countries where up to 40 percent or more of all children born did not reach the age of fifteen; there are no such countries today.

A Large Proportion of Young People and Political Turbulence

Imagine a typical less developed country with a high birthrate combined with a sharply dropping death rate. More infants survive; the result of the cohort (or age group) moving on is an expansion of the number of adolescents fifteen years later, hence more potential recruits to the labor force. An ever-growing proportion of adolescents and young adults gives the population an explosive structure. As will be explained later, many less developed countries find it difficult to invest enough to ensure proper employment for all job-seekers. The fact that a large proportion of young people are faced with the scourge of unemployment creates a tense, potentially unstable, if not explosive situation. Rural/urban migration—that is, the invasion of the cities by unemployed rural workers seeking often unavailable employment—adds to the existing tension.

The reasons why large youth cohorts easily make for social unrest are not hard to grasp. If the younger age groups grow faster than the surrounding groups of older people, the young will probably come to the conclusion that the status quo does not suit their needs and merits—which is especially true when most of the property, income, and power is in the hands of groups not actually expanding. The youthful have-nots are in a position of inferiority; their vulnerability provides an additional source of assertiveness if not aggressiveness; they are likely to exert peaceful or unpeaceful pressure on the established older generations. This situation can become the more precarious in that growing populations with more children surviving per family probably start with a "generation gap." Parents with few children are more likely to take time out to play with their children, pass on their knowledge to them, and so on. Parents of large families are likely to be more tired because they have to work harder and to want just to be left alone. The more children, the less time to devote to each and to "family life." Available evidence indicates that the number of children in the family is a very critical factor in the performance of children in school. Children of large families are at a distinct disadvantage, a result of less intensive interaction with adults. Parents of large families also seem to take less interest in the children's achievement in school.

Intergenerational pressures are also likely to increase, for another reason; if jobs are scarce, society in a way tells the youngster that he is in fact not really needed, scores of others being ready to take his place—which can lead to a venomous kind of rivalry and cutthroat competition, a desire to eliminate rivals and a general hardening of mentality. The other, more positive, side of the coin is that, if the environment is favorable and investment funds readily available, the increased competition may enliven a country's economy and lead to new initiatives, the development of new types of commodities and services, and so forth.

It is a statistically established fact that the younger age groups are more prone to engage in socially disruptive behavior than those that have passed the age of thirty. Given circumstances in which the chances of leading a fairly decent life are slim anyway, what should stop the young from turning to ideologies preaching society's demolition?

Historical Examples

It must never be forgotten that nondemographic factors may be very important and that population elements alone can never explain economic, social, and political situations, although it *does* pay to consider the population variable.

Just before the revolution broke out in 1789, France had a larger proportion of young people than at any moment thereafter; and unemployment was high. In fact, 40 percent of the population was between twenty and forty years old. As soon as revolution and wars had depleted the younger age groups, France became more quiet.

The Great Depression of the late 1920s and early 1930s hit Germany just when the ranks of young adults were the largest in that country's contemporary history, the twenty to forty-five age group forming 38.8 percent of the total population in 1925 and 41.5 percent in 1933. This was an outcrop from the high number of births that had occurred between 1900 and 1914. In the 1930 elections, 4.6 million first-time voters went to the polls, many of them young and unemployed. They gave Hitler his 107 seats in the Reichstag. To the extent that World War II reduced the proportion of young people, Germany became a different nation.

The disorders, tensions, and conflicts that characterized American society in the 1960s cannot simply be explained away by references to the Vietnam war, the poverty of certain racial and ethnic minorities, and similar factors. An important contributing factor was that the children born in the baby boom between 1940 and 1957 were coming of age. The large cohorts entering late adolescence and college age were major contributors to the social stresses and conflicts so typical of the 1960s.

The Future

Predictions are by definition notoriously hazardous. However hard we try to peer into the thick murk of the future, the results are likely to be disappointing. Yet from the particular viewpoint adopted in this chapter, it is clear that we can hardly look forward to world stability in coming decades. At present the disproportion in age structures between the developed and less developed countries is flagrant. In Western Europe there are typically between 34 and 40 persons aged from fifteen to twenty-nine for every 100 persons of thirty or over, compared with some 45 persons in the fifteen to twenty-nine group for the United States, while for the less developed countries, figures for the younger age group lie between 70 and 97. The figures for adolescents and very young adults are equally revealing. In 1960 the number of persons aged fifteen to twenty-four in the developed countries was estimated at about 24.1 percent of the population and could rise to 25.4 percent in 1980. For the less developed regions the figures are 32.4 percent (1960) and 34.1 percent (1980). The differences in reservoirs of infants and adolescents who will move with time into the older age groups are also noteworthy. In the developed countries (1970), 26.8 percent of the population was under fifteen; in the less developed countries the equivalent figure stood at 41.4 percent. The amount of young people in the latter countries is expected to soar because the number of potential parents about to enter the reproductive period is unprecedented. The presence of such large and growing proportions of youngsters, especially combined with slow economic development and concentration in urban areas, seriously increases the chances of sociopolitical stress and instability.

The Greek Philosophers on Political Stability

Interestingly, Plato and Aristotle favored population stabilization on the precise ground that continued population growth would make it impossible to maintain law, order, and democracy. However, they feared the consequences of increasing numbers with its resultant greater density of population, whereas our analysis focuses on a growing proportion of young people. Physical geography forced the Greeks to live in small city-states with a limited amount of arable land around each. The scarcity of tillable land was aggravated by population expansion and the uneven distribution of landed property. Population stabilization was advocated in order to prevent further subdivision of the land, leading to impoverishment of some citizens, discontent, and political disorder. At the same time Aristotle argued that in a larger population potential and actual rulers, on the one hand, and citizens, on the other, would no longer know each other and the system of direct democracy would break down.

The Greeks actually lived in relatively small cities; the population of free adult males in Athens, where the custom was for the citizens to meet in the marketplace to elect public administrators and discuss public affairs, probably never passed the 40,000 mark.

Do Large Populations Make Democracy Impossible?

The nation-state has now superseded the city-state, while representative democracy has replaced direct democracy. Aristotle correctly noted that opportunities for direct participation shrink in larger social and political units. The larger the community, the less one individual's impact. With 10,000 inhabitants, he represents $1/10,000$ part of the government; where there are a million citizens, his share is 1 millionth. At the same time his chances of directly communicating with political leaders like presidents or prime ministers decrease as the community grows larger. It obviously makes all the difference if you have a country inhabited by 4 million persons (United States, 1789), of whom 750,000 are slaves unable to participate in political society, or one with a population of 205 million (United States, 1970).

It might be asked whether in democratic countries democracy will be impaired by further population growth and whether expanding numbers will make its adoption more troublesome in areas not yet democratically governed. Here again there is no definite answer, and existing research is too meager to permit firm conclusions.

It may be tentatively observed that increasing numbers put democratic institutions to the test because democracy is a delicate system of government requiring constant attention, criticism, and control by the more intelligent and enlightened citizens, free debate and inquiry, and a fairly high overall level of education.

A growing population, by impairing economic progress (and hence the attainment of better levels of education), impairs democracy. Again, unemployment and the low levels of production accompanying demographic expansion may produce dictatorial measures to preserve order and guarantee minimum food supplies and other necessities.

Other effects of population expansion seem to be the complication of social institutions and proliferation of controls as production and distribution systems expand. Greater regimentation looks almost inevitable.

Finally, although direct democracy no longer exists, Aristotle's argument still holds; namely, that greater numbers lessen each citizen's prospects of communicating with his political leaders. So the inhabitants of a country become increasingly powerless and have to resort to the formation of pressure groups and/or demonstrations to make their wishes known.

5

Population explosion and population implosion

The lemon groves, the orange groves, the avocado groves, all are gone replaced by homes, houses, thousands of houses, supermarkets, in short, progress.

Senator Richard Nixon, 1951

The population explosion now taking place feeds what sociologist P. M. Hauser calls the "population implosion." What is meant by this term is the growing concentration of people on relatively small fractions of the earth's surface.

It may be useful at the outset to establish a distinction between "urbanization," defined as the rise in the proportion of the total population living in urban places, and city growth. Urbanization is a relatively recent phenomenon. On the eve of the industrial revolution, only some 2.2 percent of Europe's total population were living in urban centers of more than 100,000 inhabitants; by 1970 some 37 percent of the world's population had become urbanized; and by the year 2000 this figure will have risen to 51.1 percent. Table 4 clarifies the speed at which urbanization will proceed during the next few decades.

Table 4. *Percent of Population Urbanized*

REGION	1970	2000
World	37	51.1
More developed countries	65.7	80.7
Less developed countries	25	42.6
North America	74.2	85.1

Some figures on city growth are equally telling. From 1970 to the year 2000 the urban population in the less developed countries will triple. Before the 1970 decade is over, Calcutta may have reached the 15 million mark; Cairo will probably have at least 6 million inhabitants; and Buenos Aires 10 million; and in Latin America alone, seventeen more cities will pass the 1 million mark. The metropolitan centers of the more developed countries will experience a 66 percent growth.

The total world urban population in 1970 stood at 1.4 billion; in the year 2000 this figure will have risen to 3.3 billion. Of that total, 2.2 billion will live in the cities of the less developed countries and the remaining 1.1 billion in the urban centers of the more developed countries.

One disturbing aspect of the whole situation is that the developing countries are not repeating the experience of the more developed. In the industrialized countries of the eighteenth, nineteenth, and early twentieth centuries, city growth was mostly due to urbanization. The cities were not very healthy places to live in; urban mortality rates usually topped rural mortality; urban birthrates were relatively low. It was the continuous flow of people from rural areas into the cities that kept the cities growing. The industrial revolution in the West was accompanied by an agricultural revolution consisting of the consolidation of holdings into larger and more efficient units, advances in farming techniques, and changes in entrepreneurial attitudes. The small cultivators were often forced off the land and went to the cities to try and find employment in the newly developing industries. This evolution has permitted the development of a highly productive farming sector with a high output per man-hour plus the development of an urban industrial and service sector. In the more developed countries this transfer of human resources into the cities has continued until now, although the movement is tapering off because such a large proportion of the total population is already urbanized; hence the tempo of urbanization is declining. This does not mean that city growth has come to an end; metropolitan growth still continues (New York may well have 30 million inhabitants by the year 2010); but, countries like the United States and Britain being already nations of cities, city growth has become a function of population growth itself. In the United States the total metropolitan population increased by about 26 million people during the 1960s. About two-thirds of this metropolitan growth was due to population growth within constant boundaries; the remainder arose from rural-urban migration and immigration from abroad.

The less developed countries are also experiencing mushrooming metropolitan areas. As mentioned before, their metropolitan populations will more than treble during the last three decades of the twentieth century. The situation in these developing countries is, however, radically different from that of the more developed countries in the recent past. Both rural and urban rates of population growth are high. The city growth in the less developed countries is the result, not only of drift from the rural areas, but mainly of natural increases within city boundaries, one reason being that the death control techniques imported from the developed countries are first applied in the towns and cities, where as a result health conditions are better than in the countryside. Urban mortality is lower than rural mortality, while fertility in the cities is only slightly less than in the countryside, so that the cities in the less developed countries generate most of their own growth, which is tantamount to saying that these countries are having to face all the problems of fast metropolitan growth while the countryside often still remains crowded.

The rapid expansion of urban populations in the less developed lands is adding to their many other problems. Only too often the resources needed to provide the increasing urban populations with jobs and adequate services such as housing, education, marketing services, running water, sewerage, gas, electricity, transport are sadly lacking. Consequently, some cities are in a state of constant crisis. Unemployment and underemployment prevail, amenities are insufficient, and slum areas and shantytowns proliferate on the peripheries. Thus an ideal breeding ground for the development of personal and social disorganization is created. The underemployed, frustrated inhabitants of the urban slums who live in ugliness and poverty may well contribute to political unrest and instability. Shantytowns mushroom in most of the less developed countries. The shantytown on the outskirts of Mexico City (population 7.6 million) has become a city itself, with about 600,000 inhabitants. Some 20 percent of Caracas's 2 million inhabitants live in shacks on the surrounding hills; in Rio de Janeiro there are about 750,000 people living in shantytowns.

This is not to say that urbanization and urban growth are always undesirable. If they are combined with economic development, they are fairly worthwhile. As stated earlier, the process of urbanization in the West emptied the countryside of many low-productivity farmers; city growth enlarged markets and brought them closer to the doorsteps of firms; the higher outputs made possible or facilitated the adoption of more expensive and more productive machinery, as well as the employment and use of specialists and specialized departments. All these factors tended to cheapen products for the consumer. Besides these economies of scale, there were and are other advantages from concentration itself. Transport facilities can be improved, and workmen trained in one firm can be employed by others, thus facilitating the spread of technology, the conflux of firms in relatively restricted areas promoting the establishment of trade schools and technical colleges. But if urbanization and city growth occur without fairly rapid industrialization, unemployment and underemployment are bound to make their appearance. And if in a particular country the cities generate most of their own population growth, a problem of enormous magnitude is created.

6
Psychological effects of population density

All the world is queer save thee and me, and even thou art a little queer.

Robert Owen

What Is Population Density?

In this discussion of the psychological effects of "density" on humans, that term will be basically defined as the number of individuals per unit of space, or quantity of square inches of space per head.

While some studies take as a point of departure the number of people per unit of area, important subdivisions have been made. It does make sense to understand "density" to mean population per residential acre for cities or areas with only one-story buildings. Wherever high-rise apartment houses predominate, inches of floor space per head or "room density," i.e., average number of people per habitable room, is a more appropriate yardstick.

Although it seems that density does affect human behavior, existing research does not justify very definite conclusions. For instance, there is no doubt that there is a higher incidence of mental disorder, as manifested in alcoholism, crime rates, and attempted suicides, in the crowded city slums than in the more spacious suburbs. But is density the causative factor? The ultimate cause may well be low income or low educational levels, high migration rates, inadequate police protection, or the tendency of "societal failures" to drift into the slums—or a combination of all these factors.

There are two basic types of research about the effects of population density on living beings. Let us consider first some of the conclusions of investigations into nonhumans, then studies of humans.

Density and Nonhumans

Studies of animals are hardly restricted by ethical considerations and can be systematically controlled with relative ease. Provocative as the findings may be, they do not lead to firm conclusions about human behavior.

Many tests on animals have shown that beyond a certain point the impact of increased density is negative, well-known ones being those on Norwegian rats by Dr. John B. Calhoun. Increased crowding in cages of these rats, which were amply provided with food and medical care, produced some of the following results: the aggressive behavior of some of the male rats increased markedly; other males became completely passive and withdrew from the community; some males engaged in frenetic sexual overactivity, while some actually resorted to cannibalism, starting to eat the young; in the females there was a sharp rise in abortive pregnancy and death in pregnancy, possibly because the females were relentlessly pursued by hosts of males when they were in heat, with no way of escaping excessive attentions once the females were satisfied. Normal infant care by the females also broke down; females first began to build inadequate nests and finally no longer built nests and failed to nurse or take care of their young; nor did they defend the young when their nests were invaded by marauding males. In certain tests infant rat mortality rose to 80 percent and over. Normal courting behavior was also disrupted—in other words, the social order broke down completely.

Thus, when the density was still low, the population of the rat colony expanded rapidly, then leveled off and eventually decreased.

Studies of other rat populations and research on a variety of other animals including domestic cats have produced conclusions pretty close to those of Calhoun. A reduction of space per head inevitably seems to increase aggressive interactions, beyond a certain threshold. Alaskan lemmings whose number was constantly increased in an enclosure socialized very well up to a certain point, beyond which they became irritable and reached for each other's throats. Closer to us, primates seem to react identically.

Studies of certain small mammalian species such as mice have sometimes shown an association between rising population density and increased adrenal activity, which has led certain researchers to speculate that high density leads to stress. The stress results in increased adrenal production, which in turn produces the aggressiveness and antisocial behavior.

At the same time, the overactivation of the adrenal gland may result in higher mortality. In certain cases the rise in stress associated with greater crowding seems to overactivate the adrenal gland, with possible concomitant hypertension, arteriosclerosis, and cardiac disease—that is, higher mortality. Caged rats have been observed to drop dead because of oversecretion of adrenaline. The high incidence of pathological behavior among animal populations whose density is increased naturally leads to speculation on similar consequences for human beings.

Density and Human Population

Most of our information on humans and the effect of density on them stems basically from three types of research.

1. Demographic and survey studies measuring density in various areas, correlating results with crime rates, juvenile delinquency, admissions to mental hospitals, and so on. The trouble here is that, even if density and manifestations of social and/or personal "disorganization" turn out to be highly correlated (as they often are), the causative factor has not necessarily been discovered, since other elements besides density may be responsible.

2. Experimental studies are frequently conducted in a laboratory-like environment where the effects of density on small numbers are listed; but too often samples are small and tests last only a short while (a few hours); thus little is learned about the long-term effects of crowding.

3. Finally, observations are made in nonprefabricated environments like classrooms, hospitals, prisons; then there are the personal experiences of qualified victim-observers in such places as prison and concentration camps. Those findings have the advantage of being

arrived at in an authentic environment, though one that is uncontrolled. The ideal environment for the researcher is one where density is varied while all other factors remain constant.

Some Findings

Demographic and survey studies show rather consistently higher levels of social and personal disorganization in the most crowded areas of the big cities emerging especially from crime, attempted or "successful" suicide rates, homicide rates, outbreaks of violence, narcotic addiction, and alcoholism. In the United States, crime rates in the big cities are reportedly over five times higher than in the smaller ones, eight times higher than in the suburbs, and eleven times higher than in the countryside. Various other types of pathology do seem to accumulate in the densely crowded centers of American and English cities. The rates decline toward the periphery. Such correlational studies, however, say little about causation. For instance, research with regard to suicides seems to indicate that disturbed social relationships such as isolation and loneliness, rather than overstimulation, prompt individuals to take their lives. Such fatal gestures do occur most frequently in the crowded areas of the cities, but for some reason or another (probably because of the high migration rates) social isolation most frequently occurs right there. Mental illness as measured by mental hospital admission rates is also more prevalent in the populous city centers than in the more roomy suburbs. But this may be because in many cities the centers are deteriorated slum areas where social failures and rootless people tend to accumulate. Some positive relationship has been found between crowding per se and attempted suicides. Typically, persons making such nonfatal suicidal gestures have been tormented by high noise levels, lack of privacy, excessive demands and sensory input until their resistance failed. This occurs typically in overcrowded buildings.

Most experimental studies so far conducted consisted of putting a larger and a smaller group of men or women in identical rooms. When individuals are requested not to interact, the more crowded group feels less comfortable. When they are asked to work as a team, the men reacted negatively to crowding, but the women reacted rather positively. When groups were mixed, the difference in reaction between high- and low-density situations disappeared.

Some of the existing field and observational studies that have been made in certain housing districts, refugee camps, classrooms, factories, and the like seem to reveal that higher density produces aggressiveness and other forms of social behavior as well as psychiatric disorders. Yet there are other studies that have yielded less precise results. In explanation, it has been hypothesized that increased density usually leads to greater sensory input, hence to more stimulation. Laboratory experiments on humans have shown that overstimulation leads to high levels of adrenal output, whereas understimulation yields low levels. As with other species, different levels of adrenaline secretion seem to result in different behavioral patterns, while increased adrenal output if repeated often enough also seems to reduce resistance against disease. Yet all these findings are very tentative. It seems perhaps best to conclude by saying that the research done so far leads to a rather strong suspicion that density negatively affects human behavior. Yet there is no decisive proof. New research may lead to different conclusions.

Fertility and Crowding

With animals increased crowding reduces fertility; with humans, however, density and fertility are highly correlated—which, again, does not mean that density induces high fertility, though it may be wondered whether crowding and the resulting compulsory total involvement with the environment do not make it difficult, if not impossible, to sit back quietly and plan the future, which would include the planning of one's family. Such planning requires the ability to imagine the future and how to face it. Given a diminished orientation toward the future, the long-term implications of another child may be ill perceived; so the overcrowded may remain or become nonusers, or careless or sporadic users, of contraceptive methods. The fertility of ineffective contraceptive-users is notoriously high.

7

Population pressure, a cause of war?

Dulce bellum inexpertis. (Only to those who have never experienced it does war seem beautiful.)
Erasmus

Definition of "Pressure"

Our discussion here may well begin with a somewhat loose definition of "population pressure." It is perhaps not too far from the truth to call this a situation in which the people/resources relationship is such as to bring the standard of living far below what it would have been with a smaller population or significantly to retard economic progress.

It would be logical to argue that "population pressure" must lead to war, just as an overheated boiler with an inadequate safety valve must ultimately explode. This is, in fact, a quite common belief, one that has given rise to certain theories that, as we shall see, are no more than "tentative truths."

Theory 1: Population Pressure Makes for Hunger Wars

Overcrowding, it is argued, ultimately leads to hunger, making war the only alternative to starvation; for a population may have multiplied to the famine point, and is then left with the options of migration, death by starvation, or invasion of someone else's territory. Where peaceful migration is not possible, a hungry nation will, historically, reach out for other territories; many of history's great migrations were nothing but fights for new hunting or agricultural land. The winning tribe or community would expand, the losing tribe be enslaved or driven out—which partly explains the attacks by the Celts, Teutons, Goths, and Huns on the northern boundaries of Roman Europe. Desert Arabs, when they increased beyond their means of subsistence, raided their neighbors. When a Pacific island became too crowded, Polynesians took to their boats and colonized new islands. During the eighteenth, nineteenth, and twentieth centuries Europe was able to relieve its population pressure by sending millions of emigrants to the shores of America. The tendency is to regard this expansion into the Western Hemisphere as a peaceful and orderly process, perhaps mainly because Red Indians do not write history. Recent times (1969) show the example of a short war between Honduras and El Salvador, which was apparently attributable to population pressure. El Salvador's population was estimated at 3.3 million, its population density at 413 persons per square mile, its population density per square mile of arable land at 782, and the population growth rate at about 3 percent; hence its population was doubling about every 23 years. Honduras had a population of 2.5 million, a growth rate of about 3.2 percent, but significantly lower densities, namely, 57 per square mile and 155 per square mile of arable land. About 300,000 Salvadorans, obviously looking for land and jobs, had crossed the border during the years immediately preceding the conflict. The Hondurans began to expel them physically and armed conflict broke out, and although this was not a pure "hunger war," it is agreed that land hunger and unemployment drove the Salvadorans abroad. Our conclusion is therefore that this theory has empirical and logical support. It cannot, however, be said that differences in population density always automatically lead to international conflict.

Belgium has a higher density per square mile (317 in 1970) than West Germany (240 in 1970); but somehow, the Belgian population is not overflowing into Germany. In fact, the two countries cooperate most peacefully within the framework of the European Economic Community. Hong Kong has a density of 3,955 per square mile (1970), the figure for mainland China being 79. Yet population movement tends to be from mainland China to Hong Kong, although the migrants are usually escaping for political reasons. Examples can be multiplied indefinitely. A reverse one is that, while the United States has higher density than Canada, Canadians tend to migrate to the United States. England and Wales have eight times the density of Ireland; yet Irishmen come to England to find employment.

The reason why dense nations can do quite well, economically speaking, is that there are alternatives to armed conquest. Birth control combined with industrialization, intensification of agriculture, international trade, and encouragement of foreign investment can alleviate population pressures, at least so long as there are still other countries with surpluses of food, capital, raw materials, and minerals willing to forward these abroad.

Theory 2: Population Pressure on Resources Leads to War

This theory is closely allied to the previous one, the difference being one of emphasis rather than of kind. The gist of the argument is that with a growing population the amount of land and other resources available per head must fall, so lead to claims for additional living space (Hitler's *Lebensraum*). The high density in saturated areas breeds an attitude whereby people in neighboring countries come to be regarded as flies or mosquitoes to be got rid of. Quotable examples are the imperial efforts of England, France, and Germany after the 1870s and of Germany, Italy, and Japan in the interwar period. Some writers and rulers of these countries used the theme "colonies are to solve our population problems" in justification of foreign expansion and war. Especially in the interwar period, the fascist nations (Italy, Germany, and Japan) constantly hammered on their theme of such needs as a "place in the sun," more land and raw materials, a co-prosperity sphere. Yet it is hard to believe that those who used the "living space" type of argument were sincere. French writers, for example, who argued for imperial expansion as an outlet for people, simultaneously deplored the low birthrate in France, which was far from overcrowded during the latter decades of the nineteenth century while its colonies were if anything impoverishing the home country's taxpayer.

In the interwar period many countries experienced overpopulation from the pure self-sufficiency viewpoint; but only a few, like Italy and Germany, chose to cure it by conquest of other territories. Others, like

Switzerland, preferred such solutions as reliance on international trade. The "living space" type of reasoning has a natural advantage: it appeals to a basic sense of justice. Slogans such as "our people must have room to live in," "our children have the right to space, food, and employment" are easily understood and acted upon; often enough the fact that the expansion must take place at the expense of someone else is conveniently disregarded.

The argument used by the fascists was clearly a rationalization; the expansionist movement was stimulated and condoned by the fascist states' and their rulers' desire for power and prestige. The advantages of international adventures involving armed conflict and occupation accrue mainly to a handful of people: political leaders may gain in prestige; generals get a chance to test their ideas on the battlefield, with concomitant chances of promotion; new administrative posts are created; and speculators get new outlets for their activities. The "common man" has little to gain in all this—which is where the population argument comes in.

The winning over of the masses to costly expansionist policies demands the dinning of the *Lebensraum* argument into their ears until they really believe it and then endorse policies inimical to their own interests. Especially in a state-controlled ("totalitarian") nation, it is relatively easy to make people accept such unsound economic theories because the mass media are under state control, so that the "population pressure" argument is a cherished asset for warmongers. Great has been the past success of the trick of capitalizing on population pressure to foster expansionist policies.

Very few political scientists, historians, or other observers believe that the fascist powers were for a moment sincere in their use of the "population pressure" type of argument, because the countries that complained about their high density relative to others were doing all in their power to increase it. Emigration was discouraged, abortion and birth control were outlawed, bachelors and childless couples were heavily taxed, and marriage loans and family allowances were lavishly supplied. Moreover, tax favors were granted to large families, and prolific fathers were given preference in public employment, while the newspapers praised prolific mothers. How much farther can the urge to fertility go? Yet the Italian fascist demographer C. Gini, in *Le Rôle du Facteur Démographique dans la Politique Internationale* (Bucharest, 1941), hypocritically complained that such satisfied colonial powers as England wanted to condemn young Italians to an unmanly existence—this because it was suggested that some form of birth control is a better solution for population pressure than armed conflict and empire-building. In the same brochure Gini alluded to Italy's "natural need to expand," the "need for greater prestige in the world," Italy's "mission to affect the course of world history," and the like.

An interesting fact is that none of these countries had used whatever colonies they already had for substantial emigration, because German and Italian emigrants preferred temperate zones to the much hotter colonies in Africa and elsewhere.

By 1913, after some thirty years of colonization, there were twice as many Germans in the Bronx (New York) as in the entire German colonial empire. The Japanese equally preferred Japan to Korea or Formosa (Taiwan), which had lower-than-home standards of living.

Another interesting fact is that the areas Japan occupied in the Pacific and Southeast Asia during World War II provided only 30 percent of Japan's imports, while also proving bad markets for finished products because of their low per capita incomes.

In conclusion, it would seem that the "living space" argument, as used, was largely a rationalization. Real solutions for population pressure can and must be sought along different lines, such as reduction of birthrates, increased productivity, free trade, friendly international cooperation, and reliance on collective security, though it might be pointed out that the fascist countries received little encouragement to seek peaceful means of raising their living standards, for when the Great Depression started in 1929, most countries sought refuge in a narrow economic nationalism.

In 1930 the U.S. Congress passed the Hawley-Smoot Tariff Act, which raised already high American duties by an average of 40 percent, presenting American debtors with insoluble problems. The United Kingdom raised its tariffs in 1932 and with the empire countries adopted a system of "preferences" (mainly on tariffs) within the British Empire. Import quotas were also adopted by many countries.

Hence there was a sharp reduction in the prospect for countries like Germany, Italy, and Japan (not forgetting others) of earning the foreign exchange needed to finance imports of food and raw materials.

Another question that has recently emerged in this context is How will the United States react to the fact that by the year 2000 this country will be dependent on other countries for some 50 percent of thirty-six strategic raw materials, especially if the producing countries form commodity cartels (price arrangements that usually boost the earnings of those who enter into the agreement) such as the OPEC, or stop delivery all together?

In 1973 the Arab countries demonstrated the will and capacity to suspend trade relations and to turn off the oil tap when it fitted their purpose. There is a serious possibility that the key producers of copper, manganese, and other metals will also cartelize, boost their prices, and perhaps disrupt merchandise trade if it fits their purpose.

The United States will then face the choice of whether to change its life-style rather drastically, start a war in order to capture those strategic materials, retaliate otherwise perhaps by stopping grain deliveries, or work out a new resources diplomacy with other consuming countries. The future will show whether a peaceful solution will be found.

Theory 3: Rising Population Pressure Conducive to Political Instability?

The result of increasing population pressure may be the establishment of wrongheaded dictatorial regimes that will embark on wild adventures.

If a population grows rather rapidly and economic growth fails to catch up, a possible result is more unemployment and poverty. Examples do exist of populations whose dissatisfaction has helped to make them the dupes of mentally unstable yet charismatic demagogues. People who see little hope in other directions may contribute to the political success of power-hungry troublemakers and other persuasive men of little wisdom. Once in power, the "dictators" may be tempted by the wildest adventures; the example of Hitler obviously comes to mind.

Again, logic is on the side of this theory, although in the case of Hitler's Germany other circumstances were probably more important. The catastrophic inflation in 1922-1923 had wiped out the savings of many members of the middle class, who lost faith in the young and uncertain democracy of the Weimar Republic. The economic crises of the late 1920s and early 1930s also hit Germany especially hard because Americans withdrew their credits from Germany while many other countries closed their doors to German exports. In 1932 about 43 percent of the labor force was unemployed. Germany sank into an economic morass. This, rather than population pressure in the usual sense, plus the circumstances mentioned in Chapter 4, gave the Nazis their chance.

Theory 4: Crowding May Ultimately Lead to a Situation in Which the Instinct of Self-Preservation Will Vanish and Suicidal Mass Migrations Follow

This idea can best be illustrated by an example taken from the animal kingdom, in which there seem to exist mass migrations aimed at self-destruction and/or thinning, one of the best-known examples being the lemmings. After periods of exceptional fertility, usually due to an early spring resulting in overcrowding and insufficient resources per head, these small rodents suddenly seem to understand their desperate demographic situation and, toward the end of the summer, embark on a suicidal mass migration. The self-destructiveness of the act is evidenced by the fact that without hesitation they will rush into any obstacle in their way, including abysses, rivers, and oceans. Their normal notion of self-preservation seems to get totally lost.

Some other species, like the American squirrel and bison and the African gazelle, seem to react similarly once their density has reached certain levels—which suggests that perhaps among human beings something identical might happen once the circumstances become propitious. It is uncertain whether this inference will become a reality.

Human beings are different from lemmings, and there are many other variables to be coped with. So far as this writer knows, there is little knowledge of the circumstances in which the instinct of self-preservation could die.

Theory 5: Coexistence of High- and Low-Fertility Nations Leads to the Elimination of the Latter

It is said that high fertility in the low-income nations leads to ferocious competition among their inhabitants with a consequent hardening of the spirit. As a result of their fierce struggle for survival, the survivors will become stronger and more aggressive, while the inhabitants of the more developed, prosperous countries, with their lower fertility, will tend to soften, being ultimately overwhelmed.

This proposition is at first sight plausible; but the converse case can in fact also be argued. The malnutrition that accompanies extreme poverty seems unconducive to aggressive behavior or "survival of the fittest." It was discovered in the late 1960s that when a pregnant mother is underfed during the last three months of her pregnancy or the child during its first three months of life, the child will remain stunted for the rest of its life by brain damage.

Where part of the population is underfed, the level of vital activity will swing downward. A daily minimum of about 2,500 calories is necessary for normal productive performance; with less, people tend to become lethargic and less resistant to disease.

As population pressure increases, the tendency in many countries (especially in Asia) seems to be to rely increasingly on the consumption of the cheaper cereals like rice at the expense of protein-rich fish, poultry, and dairy products. As a lack of protein presumably diminishes health, vigor, and productive performance, the underfed/overcrowded nations are unlikely to be able to behave according to the theory here discussed.

A Residual Question: Does Population Growth Confer Proportional Power on a Country?

Allied with this question are many others. It has been said, for instance, that since the populations of Africa, Asia, and Latin America are now growing and will in the future grow faster than those of the Western world, Japan, and the Soviet Union, the balance of power will shift against the latter.

All we can safely say, however, is that in the past, population size and political power were probably more highly correlated than now. In the past, power in international relations largely depended on the armies a nation could bring into the field, and since military personnel are drawn from restricted age groups, the volume of population conditioned the nation's army. But even then, mere numbers were far from decisive. The fact that European nations were able to overrun and colonize such large territories and populations in Africa, Asia, and elsewhere was mainly due to their better firepower and technology. Numerically the colonizers were inferior. In World War I, Germany was able to beat Russia despite that country's greater numbers. The Russian army was more poorly trained and equipped. In the 1967 war between Egypt and Israel the Egyptians alone outnumbered the Israelis by 12 to 1. Paramount in purely military terms are the stage of economic growth, per capita income, the level of application of technology to a nation's resources, the availability of specialists, motivation, government efficiency, and access to raw materials.

Numbers alone do not necessarily confer military weight. The large and growing populations of so many low-income countries may turn out to be a source of military weakness, because they prohibit or significantly retard the formation of human and physical capital, modernization, and other trends. Moreover, poverty may simply prevent a nation from bearing the costs of preparation for war, or the expense of a sustained war. The confrontation between India and Pakistan in 1972 broke down after a short while because neither side could afford more fighting. Their economies were on the verge of collapse.

Now that wars can be fought with atomic weapons, the prospects of destruction have become so great that perhaps it no longer makes much sense to think in terms of classical armies fighting with rifles and tanks, although small local wars are likely to recur.

How much power does population guarantee under peaceful conditions? At present the United States has more power than India, whose population is more than two and one-half times as large. Sweden, with nearly 8 million inhabitants (1970), seems to have more persuasive power in international relations than Nigeria with over 55 million inhabitants. Once more, mere numbers do not seem conclusive. Per capita income, the state of the arts, a nation's institutional apparatus, the educational level of the population—these factors are as important as, if not more important than, sheer numbers.

In conclusion, will the balance of power shift against the West as a result of the shift of population centers of gravity? This question can hardly be answered with precision. The higher fertility of the less developed countries may just as easily work against them and cause collapse, internal turmoil, and disintegration. The future will, however, require great statesmanship of the West for the reason that population pressure is sure to rise enormously in most countries. This need not result in war, but will most probably increase the chances of

armed conflict. The chances of enduring peace will be greatly
enhanced by a policy of restraint, a friendly spirit of international
cooperation, a more understanding attitude toward other peoples,
and intelligently conceived aid by the more prosperous developed
countries.

8

Economics and population growth

> *If the world would not be so full of people and most of them did not have to work so hard, there would be more time for them to lie on the grass, and there would be more grass for them to lie on.*
>
> Don Marquis

An Old Preoccupation

Since the economists have been discussing the implications of population for more than two centuries, quite a solid body of knowledge has by now been built up. Here, however, we can do no more than scratch the surface of the subject and present some conclusions.

The first name that springs to mind in this context is that of the British economist Thomas Robert Malthus (1766-1834). His theory was that population, if not somehow checked, tends to increase faster than available food supplies, with inevitable hardship to follow. In the long run, man faces the dramatic alternative between controlling population growth ("preventive" check) and starvation ("repressive" check). Malthus's favorite solution was late marriage, to shorten the reproductive period and thus reduce families to only a few children. The essence of his ideas had already been expressed by many of his precursors. The Italian economist Giammaria Ortes (1712-1790) especially had strongly argued that on a finite earth, population growth can only be a temporary phenomenon; but even earlier economists had recognized that population growth sometimes carries certain advantages, which we shall now discuss.

Population Growth Permits a Better Division of Labor

While a small and insulated economy is likely to be characterized by rather crude and inefficient methods of production, increased population allows an enlarged community to benefit from what we call the economies of large-scale production—a phenomenon that can be analyzed at two levels.

The high efficiency of large modern business firms derives substantially from specialization by the labor force in sharply defined tasks in which the workers acquire great dexterity in the use of sophisticated equipment and tools. Commodities are thus produced in large quantities at low unit cost. This a small population with a small domestic market cannot achieve. Mass production industries will fail to emerge if there are not enough customers to purchase their output. Hence it is growing markets that foster the establishment of efficient mass production industries, although it should be noted that participation in international trade can compensate for a small domestic market; Switzerland, for example, enjoys all the advantages of large-scale production of watches despite its relatively small population. The development of cheap and rapid communications also tends to reduce the population density needed for efficient production, because division of labor and specialization become feasible and profitable even with a rather sparse population. During the nineteenth century, the construction of the U.S. railroads joined the many and varied parts of that vast country into a unified market where even the back doors of manufacturers and wholesalers could be quickly reached.

An essential condition for population growth to have the cost-reducing effects described above is that the growing quantum of customers be equipped with sufficient purchasing power to convert their needs and desires into effective demand.

For the economy as a whole, larger populations apparently facilitate the execution of large-scale, expensive, and labor-consuming projects like the construction of bridges, canals, railways, and roads, whereas in small communities there is neither the demand nor the resources for such costly projects.

Population Growth Reduces the Penalty of Errors in Investment

When population growth is fairly rapid, a wrong investment resulting in a temporary oversupply of a particular commodity or service is soon corrected because of the steadily expanding market. By reducing the penalty for miscalculations, increased population favors further new investments by firms, industrialists, and merchants, although it should be added that a stationary prospering population may be fitter to absorb a growing volume of commodities resulting from investment than may be an increasing population with little purchasing power. It cannot be denied, however, that a growing population combined with rising incomes creates an ideal climate for further new investments.

Increased Flexibility

A fairly rapid population expansion must inevitably increase the proportion of young people, whose attitudes may be more flexible and more open to reform, the learning of new skills, innovation, initiative, and creativity—which may positively affect willingness to take risks and establish new firms.

Again, the entire labor force will probably become more adaptable as young people come in, finding it easier to change jobs than do the old, thus facilitating the expansion of new industries that can always secure an adequate supply of workers.

Where, however, increasing population reduces the quality of education and training, the advantage of the greater adaptability of the labor force is offset by lower all-round skills. We now turn from some of the advantages of population growth to some of the adverse implications.

Worsening Relationship Between Physical Resources and the Human-Production Factor

One effect of population growth is to increase the labor force, although with a time lag. The question is: Will output increase at least proportionally with the labor supply? Labor is but one production factor. Only if the other resources like land, raw materials, and capital (productive equipment) are expanded concurrently, can output be expected to increase proportionally. If land, raw products, or equipment grow less rapidly than the labor force, per capita output is bound to diminish because each member of the labor force has fewer nonhuman resources to work with, *ceteris paribus* of course. In fact, other things have in many cases not remained equal. In numerous countries, like the United States, economic "organization," which includes, for instance, management efficiency and technological progress toward better products and production methods, works in the opposite direction by raising productivity and offsetting the decline in landed resources per head, whereas capital assets also accumulate at a higher rate than population. In this context it should be noticed that land resources can hardly be expanded at all, except, as in the Netherlands, only in limited amounts and at extravagant costs. Man-made capital resources such as factories or office buildings can be expanded, but only if the required investment funds are available. For the nation as a whole, capital-building means that production factors are used to make equipment rather than consumer goods; so the real sacrifice in adding to the capital stock lies in foregoing such goods. As for raw materials, their quantity shrinks constantly as they are used up; countries offset shrinkage by importing, but in the very long term worldwide exhaustion is inevitable. In fact, many of the more developed countries, like Japan, the United Kingdom, and other West European countries, have come to depend more and more on international trade to acquire the fuels and raw materials needed to compensate for their absence or growing scarcity at home. The United States is also increasingly committed to the import of foreign fuels, minerals, and other raw materials.

Population Growth and Foreign Trade in the More Developed Countries

A glance at a few typical developed countries, like Japan, the United Kingdom, Germany, and perhaps Hong Kong, shows them to be densely populated and short of agricultural land, raw materials, and fuels, yet able to enjoy fairly high standards of living, although rather hopelessly overpopulated from the self-sufficiency angle. They pay for their imports with foreign exchange earnings obtained by exporting manufactured commodities produced by a skilled, versatile, and well-equipped labor force. The system works well as long as there are countries rich in tillable land and other physical resources and willing to export food and raw materials, and so long as the land-poor countries can find markets for their industrial products. They pay for their prosperity through their vulnerable economic system; for a densely populated land-poor country is mortgaged to a wide variety of circumstances it cannot, or can barely, control. What if the extractive industries' costs begin to increase for the suppliers of raw materials? What if countries like Canada, Australia, and the United States, with their steady food surpluses, begin to fill up? What if more and more nations including the land-rich ones increasingly turn to the processing of their own raw materials? What if the producers of fuels demand even more extravagant prices for oil deliveries? What will be the fate of the land-poor nations in periods of economic nationalism, protectionism, and international conflicts that might lose them their markets or sources of supply? Their delicate economic organization would be disrupted. Yet such awkward questions must be asked. Even the United States is going to face them. Until recently its economy has been close to being self-sufficient, but it is now forced by progressive exhaustion of fuels and other nonrenewable mineral resources to put increasing pressure on foreign resources—which is bound to mean greater dependence on others and less room for maneuver in international relations. We shall simply have to accept unfriendly behavior from a nation if it happens to be a big oil supplier. In 1973 the United States was still able to protect Israel when during the fourth war with its Arab neighbors the USSR supplied Egypt and Syria with arms. In that year the United States got only 8 percent of its oil from the Middle East, thus remaining able to take a strong stand with the Arab nations, while at the same time the European nations were getting 85 percent of *their* oil needs from the same source, so had no choice but to dissociate themselves from U.S. support of Israel and to go through shameful contortions to get on the good side of the Arabs. What the Arab oil producers learned during the Yom Kippur war was that they can blackmail at least part of the Western world. The lesson is not likely to be forgotten, and it may well be that other producers of some key raw material will try to get together and do the same thing.

Further population growth in the relatively prosperous but land-poor nations such as the Netherlands, Japan, and the United Kingdom tends to have a negative effect on their balance of payments (usually defined as a nation's annual record of transactions with the outside world), for the reason that almost all the additional food and raw materials needed by the swollen populations has to be imported, while simultaneously the new raw materials needed to produce the extra exports required to pay for the extra imports must also be obtained from abroad.

Reliance on foreign trade to offset domestic scarcity of food and raw materials may also provoke balance-of-payments problems in the less developed countries; before discussing this we shall, however, turn to other issues.

Wastefulness of High Birth and Death Rates in the Less Developed Countries

There are still a number of countries where both birth and death rates are high. Most of them are in Africa, some in Asia. Examples are Portuguese Guinea (death rate 30 per thousand), Upper Volta (29 per thousand), Sikkim (29 per thousand), and Afghanistan (27 per thousand). Although such high death rates may temper the general population increases, we are facing a situation that is economically (and otherwise) wasteful. Much of the effort, and means, invested in the upbringing, education, and training of children is squandered because many of them never reach the prime of life and never join the labor force.

All investments, material, immaterial, in children who die before becoming productive, are, literally, a dead loss. In India, for instance, (early 1950s) about 20 percent of the national income was devoted on children who died before age fifteen anyway. Then there are the indirect losses, like the time the mother "wasted" on the child, maternal mortality, and the exhausting effects of repeated pregnancies.

Sharp Rise in Nonproductive Dependents

The commonest situation in the less developed countries is a combination of high birthrates and plummeting death rates, which result in substantial net population increases. In 1971 Thailand, for instance, had a crude birthrate of 41 per thousand people and a crude death rate of 11 per thousand, resulting in a rate of natural increase of 3 percent. A typical short-term (20 to 25 years) effect of improved "survivorship" is the sharp rise in the number of nonworkers ("inactive consumers" or young dependents). These young people (fifteen years of age, or under) must be fed, clothed, housed, and educated, while making little or no contribution to production. In the less developed countries, it is not uncommon to find 40 to 45 percent of the population to be under fifteen years of age.

In the more developed countries, half that figure is more typical. In Mexico (1972) 46 percent of the total population was under fifteen years old; Costa Rica (1968) has 127 children under fifteen to every 100 adults (twenty to fifty-nine years old); Denmark (1968) has 46 children per 100 adults. Large families with many unproductive youngsters make it more difficult for women to find work outside the home (or even to work in the fields if they happen to live on a family farm), so in that sense large families reduce the size of the active population.

The existence of a large proportion of persons below working age also makes saving and investment, hence economic growth, more difficult. When families are large, the cost of bringing up the children tends to encroach on what could otherwise be savings; for the more children there are in a household, the greater the pressure to spend on consumption.

A decline in fertility would release more funds for investment, and thus increase output per head. A high proportion of young dependents also curbs the government's powers to tax and borrow from the population in order to finance public investments in such projects as transport facilities, power, irrigation, soil conservation, or—on the social side—hospitals, sanitation, and education.

Fast Rise in Numbers Impedes Capital Formation

We come, in passing, to the medium-term (20 to 60 years) effects of population expansion. The high-fertility countries witness a steady increase in recruits to their labor forces, and hence rising investment requirements. Additional workers need more output-producing equipment (tools, machinery, plant) in industry, agriculture, or the service sector. If the existing amount of capital per worker—and, therefore, his productivity—are to be safeguarded, each new recruit to the labor force must be guaranteed the same amount of real capital assets. Population growth, with its concomitant increase in the labor force, swells investment needs. The simplest way to calculate the investment levels required to cover population growth is the following.

A 1 percent increase in population would require a 1 percent increase in the gross national product (GNP) to maintain per capita output or income. The value of the capital stock in many countries has been estimated at about three times the GNP—which means that it takes three dollars of productive equipment to produce one dollar of output. If we assume that it also takes three dollars in investment to increase the GNP by one dollar, a 1 percent increase in population requiring a 1 percent expansion of GNP, to prevent a fall in per capita income, would call for a 3 percent investment rate. A 3 percent growth in population (by no means uncommon in many less developed countries) would require 9 percent of the national income to be saved and invested just to hold per capita incomes at previous levels. Running hard to stay on the spot. Colombia, with a population growth rate of 3.4 percent (1973), must, we reckon, invest annually around 14 percent of its GNP if it is to absorb population and labor increases and, at the same time, hold per capita income to a constant level. Countries like Thailand or Morocco must invest around 9 percent annually, merely to stop capital per head from declining. In countries like the Philippines, Malaysia, and the United Arab Republic, the proportion of this "waste" of national income lies between 7.5 and 10 percent, while for the United States and Western Europe in general it is less than 3 percent, and obviously, for a nation with a stationary population, 0 percent.

To save 7.5 to 10 percent of any GNP takes a major effort. Again, all less developed countries want "intensive" economic development, because they wish to raise per capita production or the standard of living—which requires what the economists call "capital deepening" or, quite simply, more capital per worker.

High fertility is therefore a major constraint on the use of more capital per worker, because growth of the labor force absorbs nearly all domestic savings, leaving little for "capital deepening." In other words, population growth either prevents or greatly retards improved standards of living in the less developed countries—a situation the developed countries have never known to the same degree. Between 1900 and 1950 the population of Western Europe increased at an average annual rate of 0.6 percent. During the nineteenth century growth rates were lower in the West than now in most less developed countries, whereas Western Europe's birthrates never exceeded 40 per thousand—a much lower figure than in a number of less developed countries.

The Less Developed Countries and International Trade

Assume that a group of developing countries succeed both in investing enough to keep pace with their population growth and increasing labor force and in investing in improved standards of living, and also that their populations increase by some 3 percent per annum. The labor force is assumed to grow at the same pace, while the GNP grows somewhat faster. Could this situation be perpetuated for any length of time? Doubtful! For supplies of land and natural resources are fixed. As raw materials are used up, the available amounts shrink. Continued population growth implies that the per capita amount of arable land declines as well, time making the group of countries we had in mind ever more deficient in landed resources. Thus, in order to provide food, income, and employment for their growing numbers, such nations would be forced into far-reaching structural reorganization of their economies, having to produce and export more and more labor-oriented products against imported food and raw materials.

As more and more countries may be expected to follow suit, terms of trade are likely to become ever harder for the exporters of labor-oriented commodities in the sense that a given quantity of manufactured products would probably buy a steadily diminishing quantity of raw materials or food. Balance-of-payments deficits may turn up at this stage—when our imaginary group of countries would be faced with five unattractive options: (1) wages might have to be reduced in order to become more competitive on world markets; (2) "capital-deepening" investments might have to be stepped up to increase labor productivity; (3) import duties might be raised or quotas introduced to reduce imports (though these might provoke retaliatory action); (4) export subsidies could be introduced, but would have to be taken out of government funds otherwise devoted to education, highways, and the like; and (5) the currency might be devalued to cheapen the country's exports—with the concomitant problem of raising the cost of vital imports of food and raw materials. All the options seem to imply a lower living standard.

Distribution of Income

When a country's labor force grows rapidly relative to land and capital as is the case in many less developed countries, the sharper competition among tenant farmers and sharecroppers for land raises land rents while keener bidding for money capital increases interest rates. As more and more workers vie for scarce jobs, wages are likely to decline. Hence the incomes of land and property owners rise, and those of wage earners fall. Under the law of supply and demand, the largest class is by definition the weakest. The prices of commodities and production factors, such as labor, tend to equate supply and demand. With a rapidly growing labor force, the price of labor (i.e., wages) tends to drop until all labor is hired. From the strictly economic viewpoint, this is a desirable situation. Declining wages encourage employers to economize on relatively scarce and expensive resources such as land and equipment and to use more of the abundant and relatively cheap resource, such as labor. Declining wages, however, especially when they are already low, clash with the ideal of social justice and increase social tensions; although then, if governments and/or trade unions try to maintain or increase wages, firms will not absorb the whole labor force—which raises the level of unemployment and leads to frustration, both sowing the seeds of social conflict.

In a country like the United States, population growth also redistributes income so that people wishing to buy or rent a house or apartment find their real incomes reduced by soaring land prices, the proportion of their incomes which must be devoted to obtaining adequate shelter rising continuously. The winners in the lottery are the real-estate owners. The total market value of all taxable land in the United States rose from $401 billion in 1962 to $780 billion in 1972—which dramatically affected the cost of homesites, which doubled between 1961 and 1971. With a growing population, the demand for land swells steadily while the supply remains fixed; thus prices are bound to soar.

Subdivision of the Land

In many (especially Asian) less developed countries, growing rural density leads to excessive fragmentation of the land—which is especially bad for subsistence farmers, who are largely outside the cash economy. When a farmer dies, his land is subdivided among his, generally, numerous sons. A small holding impoverishes the cultivator and prevents him from saving to improve his farm or buy equipment and/or fertilizers. A side effect is that the owner of a tiny farm cannot save anything against emergencies (bad harvest for instance), which forces him to borrow when they arise. The farmer's only collateral is his land; if he fails to repay his loan from the village moneylender, his land is claimed, whereupon he sinks to the level of a sharecropper or rural proletarian.

In Thailand, for instance, it has been estimated that the average amount of arable land per farmer will be cut in half between 1970 and 1990. The present average amount of land per farmer is about 3 acres. It will decline to 1.64 acres by 1990.

Conclusion

While some of the effects of population growth are positive, there are few, if any, countries left where the negative effects do not more than outweigh whatever benefits more growth in numbers may entail.

9

Men and food

Is the Race Between Food and Population Being Lost?

The one thing certain about man is that the problem of obtaining enough food has plagued him since life began. Mankind's history has been a continuous race between humans and food, a race often lost. Famines dramatically adjust the population of a given area to available food supplies. They occurred regularly and universally in the past. Between A.D. 1000 and the nineteenth century, France was ravaged by 150 serious ones, one every six years on the average. From 1200 to 1500 there were an average of seven famines to the century in England. Asia has been and may well become again the traditional seat of famines. The following description of the great famine of 1630-1631 in India, by a European onlooker called Von Twist, realistically depicts the face of famine.

In towns and villages, in fields and on roads, men lay dead in great numbers, causing a horrible stench. For want of grass, cattle fed on the corpses. Men took the carcasses of beasts to eat; some in desperation went about searching for bones which had been gnawed by dogs. As the famine spread, men abandoned towns and villages and wandered about aimlessly. It was easy to recognize their condition: eyes sunk deep in the head, lips pale and covered with slime, the skin hard, with the bones showing through, the belly nothing but an empty pendulous pouch, knuckles and kneecaps showing prominently. One would cry and howl from hunger, while another lay stretched on the ground dying in misery; wherever you went, you saw nothing but corpses. Men deserted their wives and children, women sold themselves as slaves, mothers sold their children, children deserted by their parents sold themselves. Some families took poison to die together; others drowned themselves. Mothers and their children would go to the rivers and drown, hand in hand; so the rivers flowed with corpses. Some ate carrion; others eviscerated corpses to fill their own bellies; even men lying still alive in the streets were cut up by others; thus men fed on living men, so that even in the street, and more so on road journeys, men ran the risk of being murdered and devoured.

The question arises: Will famines recur? The answer is that they are still with us and that they will spread unless we halt population growth.

In the fall of 1974, at least 460 million people were threatened with starvation from hunger. Most of those people live in India, Bangladesh, in the zone south of the Sahara, and in such Latin American countries as Colombia, Ecuador, and Peru. In Dacca, the capital city of Bangladesh, street sweepers each morning clean the gutters of dozens of dead bodies. Indian newspapers report that entire families have committed suicide in order to end the agony of slow death by starvation. In a number of other countries, the situation is hardly any better.

The present fix, however, is not merely a result of long-term growing population. Between 1968 and 1970, the three major grain exporters (the United States, Canada, and Australia) clipped their tilled acreage by respectively 20, 50, and 40 percent. These cutbacks were induced by national authorities of these countries as a response to a situation of falling prices and growing surpluses, which was characteristic of the mid-1960s. Since 1970 these policies have been reversed, but after that date the world was plagued by bad weather and crop failures that reduced supplies and drove up prices.

The Present Situation

Most discussions of the food problem make a useful distinction between (1) undernourishment or hunger and (2) malnutrition. "Undernourishment" means insufficient calorie intake, the average adult requirement being a minimum of about 2,400 calories a day. "Malnutrition" means an inadequate intake of proteins, fat, minerals, or vitamins, often caused by a monotonous, starchy diet.

Some 10 to 15 percent of the world's population is undernourished (1970). About 1.5 billion people suffer from malnutrition (1970). Most of the undernourished and malnourished people live in Asia, Africa, and Latin America. The total annual number of deaths in the world is estimated at about 60 million. Some 10 to 20 million deaths are due to hunger or malnutrition. And each year over 70 million extra mouths have to be fed.

Undernourishment and Malnutrition Are Undesirable

This sounds much like a truism. Yet policy around the world seems pretty loath to give the solution of the food problem top priority. We all recognize that adequate food in both quantity and quality is essential to human vitality and happiness. Deficiency in food leads to lethargy, weakness, and indifference, and so to low productivity. Hunger leads to frustration, unrest, and aberrant thinking and can conduce to revolution and war.

Shortage of proteins, vitamins, and minerals reduces resistance to infectious diseases; in certain areas of Southeast Asia some 40 percent of all children die in their first four years, mostly of infectious diseases, the fact being that malnutrition has often so debilitated their bodies that they can no longer effectively resist infections. Protein hunger leads to irreversible brain damage in infants; prenatal malnutrition has the same effect; the children affected remain stunted for the rest of their lives.

Protein hunger also causes specific deficiency diseases, like *kwashiorkor*, a common disease among young children (one to six years old) of the low-income countries, whose protein requirements are not satisfied by the starchy diet on which they often live, to become victims of this terrible disease, which manifests itself in muscular disintegration, skin sores, liver degeneration, and finally death. Vitamin A deficiency frequently results in eye diseases, if not total blindness. In India alone there are estimated to be about a million cases of blindness caused through lack of vitamin A.

How much food there is and will be for each person depends on two factors, namely, total demand and total supply of farm products. A closer look at these two magnitudes will give us a better idea of what to expect in the years to come.

The Demand for Food

Two forces are responsible for expanding food needs: population growth and increased per capita income. As population grows, food production has to be pushed up in order to maintain existing consumption levels. This is sometimes called the "population effect." "Income effect" means that, given rising incomes, per capita consumption of farm produce may be expected to increase because people have more to spend.

Based on the experience of the 1960's, world population is thought to be increasing by 2 percent per annum. In many less developed countries population is, or will soon be, rising at 2 to 3 percent. A population that increases by 3 percent doubles every twenty-three years and multiplies eighteen-fold in a century. Most of the 3 billion people that will be added to the world population by the end of the century will be living in the less developed countries, while in the developed countries population will be growing by around 1 percent or less. The world "population effect" will be about 2 percent, while the world "income effect" is estimated at about 1.8 percent. Per capita income in the developed countries has been estimated to keep rising at about 3.6 percent per year; for the less developed the figure is around 2.4 percent—which amounts to a world average of 3 percent. The income elasticity of demand for food—that is, the reaction of demand to changes in income—for the developed countries lies between 0.2 and 0.3 percent. (An income elasticity of demand for food of 0.2 percent means that if incomes rise by 1 percent, the demand for food rises by 0.2 percent.) For the less developed countries, income elasticity of demand for food is estimated at 0.6 to 0.95 percent. Such higher figures are due to the lesser extent to which present food needs are satisfied; consequently, a larger proportion of the increments in income will be spent for adequate food. Global income demand elasticity would be about 0.6 percent. If global income rises by 3 percent annually and world income demand elasticity is 0.6 percent, then the aggregate "income effect" will be 3 x 0.6 percent = 1.8 percent.

The combined population and income effect is 2 percent + 1.8 percent = 3.8 percent, which implies a doubling in some eighteen years. Between the years 1973 and 2009, food requirements will have doubled twice, the fact being that never in history has agriculture had to face such increases in demand.

Even in terms of grain alone, this leads to some interesting figures. Just before World War II the less developed countries still exported some 11 million tons of grain (mostly to Europe). Their import requirements in 1970 stood at about 11.4 million tons. Estimates for 1980 are 39.4 million tons and for 2000, 153.3 million tons.

Food Supplies

Can such increases in demand as described above be met? Before attempting to answer this question, we might consider whether we are not perhaps asking the wrong kind of question. Calculating how many people the earth can feed amounts to inquiring what maximum population the planet can bear. "Maximum" population is always bad for any country as well as for the world as a whole. Once it is reached, men are standing with their backs to the wall. A succession of bad harvests will have people starving in the streets. What really matters is the "optimum" size of population, that is, the total that will give men the highest "welfare," broadly defined. That the optimum is far below the maximum is evident. It has been estimated at about 2.5 billion for the world as a whole and is already far behind us. Gloomy as calculations about the maximum are, however, they are not without interest and they lead to other important questions.

The "Good Earth"

The world map of land utilization is quite well established. The total land area of the world is about 37 billion acres, including Antarctica, minus which we have some 32 billion acres left. This figure includes the cold margin where the mean temperature for the three summer months falls below 55° F., and the arid margin where rainfall is extremely limited or where the degree of evaporation is high. The cold margin, about one-fifth of the total, is unsuitable for cereals and similar crops but can produce some hay. The arid margin, about two-fifths of the total, consists mostly of desert land, some of which can be used for sparse grazing of cattle, sheep, and goats. Of what remains, about one-fifth is used for crop production. These are the best lands, where the costs per unit of product are the lowest. Nearly all of them were already in use before World War II. The other four-fifths are used for grazing, forestry, and the like. These are the high-cost lands; they are too dry, too wet, too hilly, too stony, too heavy, or too light for successful cultivation of present prices. Expansion of crop area in the United States as well as in the world as a whole will be at the expense of the best of these lands. Summing up we have the results shown in Table 5. Some continents have larger reserves than others. Europe and Asia have the smallest reserves, as Table 6, a summary of areas that could be but are not cultivated, shows.

It should, however, be remembered that in respect of climate, environment temperature, fertility, and distance from markets these remaining lands are much inferior to those already cultivated. At the same time urbanization and industrialization encroach gradually on arable land that is often of good quality.

Table 5. *Total Land Area by Use (1960s)*

LAND	ACRES (BILLIONS)*
World	32 to 33
Built-on area as well as arid and cold margin	13.5 to 16
Usable	16 to 18.5
Used for cropping	3 to 3.6
Meadows and pastures in use or potential	5.4 to 6.8
Forest and woodland	9.9

Figures are rough approximations and do not tally.

Table 6. *Land Reserves by Region (1970s)*

AREA	RESERVES OF LAND (MILLION ACRES)*
Europe	90
Asia	270
North America	560
Latin America	1,490
Africa	1,420
USSR	320
Australia and New Zealand	340

Figures are rough approximations and do not tally.

Expansion of Utilized Acreage

One method of increasing world food supplies is to expand the cultivated area. Between 1967 and 1982, the demand for grain alone will expand by 500 million tons or 50 percent of present production. It will be necessary to use more land. If, as the figures in Table 5 show, only one-fifth of the usable acreage is cropped, the impression is created that food supplies could probably be considerably enlarged if only more lands were taken up. In Europe and Asia there is not much arable land left and whatever remains cannot be profitably cropped at present food prices.

The largest reserves are obviously in Africa and Latin America. The Amazon Valley has attracted considerable attention because of its huge dimensions (two-fifths of the entire continent of South America); but the soil in this area is only moderately fertile and is thin, deriving its fertility mainly from decayed vegetation. Clearing this land, which itself would be very costly, would destroy the soil's major source of fertility, the forest. The heavy tropical rains are likely to provoke erosion once the trees are gone and the soil broken up. Drainage, soil conservation techniques, and lavish use of plant nutrients like calcium, magnesium, potassium, and phosphorus will be needed to maintain the soil's fertility. Cultivation costs would be extremely high. The same holds for the tropical rain forests in the Congo River basin.

There is also hope that the semiarid savannahs of northern

Australia, Latin America, and Africa can be used for more intensive livestock production or cropping. Here the water supply is limited to one period of the year. Annual differences in rainfall are great. During the hot season the soil becomes hard like stone, whereas during the rainy season the land is flooded so that the essential nutrients leach downward and as a result these soils have become lateritic, being composed mainly of iron oxides and aluminum. Fertilizers can be supplied but only from long distances, even from other countries. Aside from the need for foreign exchange, this would require the construction of railways or suitable roads. The farmers would have to be taught how to maintain the soil, and credit facilities would have to be made available. The regularization of water supplies would involve the problem of finding sources of water such as rivers and lakes and distributing the water. The latter implies the construction and maintenance of expensive irrigation works, and the transport of water over long distances requires large amounts of local energy supplies.

The United States itself has some 50 million acres still unused. Most land was formerly cultivated but was later abandoned. It can be brought back into production, but only if food prices are higher than now, to cover future higher farming costs. The costs per unit of agricultural product on the land now in the soil bank will be higher because of relatively low quality. Examples of land still available in the United States are the hills of New England and the Appalachians and the poorly drained areas of Iowa.

Some encroachment by agriculture on the northern forests in Canada, the Soviet Union, and Scandinavia is possible, although these forests should not be lightly destroyed. The softwood timber they supply is used for building, fuel, and paper production. Timber exports pay Canada, Sweden, Finland, and the Soviet Union handsome incomes. It has been estimated that nevertheless some 10 percent of those forest lands could be used for cropping and somewhat more for livestock farming. The main problems are long winters (250 days of snow cover) and poor surface drainage. The melting of the snow in spring and the insufficient evaporation of summer precipitation create almost insoluble waterlogging problems. Massive drainage would be required to turn potentially usable areas into cropland.

Most continents have desert areas, which are by some considered to have a food-yielding potential. Annual rainfall in the deserts of North Africa, Australia, the Middle East, and the United States is less than ten inches. Only with irrigation will some crops grow. Here and there the problem is water distribution. Given sources, water can be brought to dry areas, but only by heavy prior investments in dams, canals, tunnels, pipelines, and ditches. Elsewhere even total catchment in a region would not give enough water for all potentially arable land. The Colorado Basin is such a case.

Desalination of ocean water is still very expensive, though now carried out in places like Kuwait with cheap power supplied by locally produced oil.

Experiments have, however, shown that in certain cases salt water can be used for irrigation and soils consisting of unconsolidated sand dune or gravel can, with it, produce certain fruits and vegetables.

Another line of experiment has shown that the spraying of desert land with a petroleum mulch can increase its fertility considerably. Theoretically, technology can develop much of the presently unused lands; yet the fact remains that these are all problem areas requiring very substantial investment—about $2,000 for each extra acre—and results are uncertain.

Increasing the Productivity of Now Cultivated Areas

Many observers have noted the unwisdom of placing much hope on yields from land presently unused. Man's best chance of meeting future food requirements apparently lies in increasing per acre yields from land already under cultivation. A precondition here is a halt to depletion and destruction of good farmland.

Erosion and Destructive Utilization

Most of man's food is produced in a thin layer of topsoil. Denuding the land of its natural cover of forest or grass and using it for agriculture exposes the soil mantle to erosion by water or wind; that is, the fertile topsoil is washed into rivers or oceans or just blown away. Continued monoculture has reduced the fertility of certain soils. It might have been expected that man would carefully manage the good land he so much depends on; but in fact that is barely true. North Africa, once a major granary of the Roman Empire, is today but a hostile, infertile desert. (The Sahara Desert itself is still increasing by 40,000 acres a year.)

In the United States, at least 100 million acres have been destroyed beyond repair; about 60 percent of all cropland is in need of conservation treatment. Every year a million acres are ruined by erosion; the dust storms in 1935, which clouded the sky in Washington, D.C., called attention to the tragic results of soil destruction. The Soil Erosion Act of 1935 and subsequent legislation may have improved the situation; but soil erosion still continues.

The rest of the world is not doing much better. In Asia, the Middle East, North Africa, and Central America, millions of acres of cropland are lost annually. Twenty-five percent of the tilled land in India will loose its topsoil before the end of this century, according to soil surveys. Nature, of course, also produces topsoil through the weathering of rock, but it takes several centuries to form one inch of it.

Mismanagement of the soil has taken other forms besides careless cropping. Flood irrigation over flat land without adequate drainage raises water tables; the land is finally saturated, and salts accumulate in the topsoil; the water nearest to the surface evaporates, leaving a salt deposit. It has been suggested that the ancient civilizations of the Near East thus lost their life-supporting agricultural basis.

Overexploitation of forests has sometimes changed the climate of an area for the worse. Overgrazing has sometimes caused the loss of better pasture species.

To stop erosion the following measures are essential.

1. Land should be fallowed to accumulate moisture, though this is almost impracticable in the densely populated less developed countries (Asian nations especially), which cannot afford this luxury.
2. Farms should be landscaped (contour farming), with trees planted at crucial spots where erosion might be gravest. When alternate strips are plowed and planted, wind erosion is almost entirely eliminated, and sheet erosion and gully erosion are also abated.
3. Planting of windbreaks.
4. Reforestation.
5. Controlled grazing of cattle to avoid overgrazing.
6. Crop rotation (mixed cropping and animal husbandry or mixed grass-legume pastures).

The problem with the first four is their cost. Can farmers and governments in low-income countries afford these solutions? Procedures 5 and 6 require farmer training.

Agricultural Reforms

In many countries, the forms of land tenure and land distribution result in low productivity per acre. In much of Latin America, for example, much of the land is owned by huge private estates called *latifundios* on which there may be little (extensive) or no cultivation. Half the agricultural land in Latin America consists of holdings of more than 15,000 acres. Because of their wealth, the rich landowners have little incentive to use the land more intensively and great areas are devoted to cattle ranching and hunting. In most of Latin America, moreover, ranching enjoys more prestige than cropping; hence much good land is merely left to pasture or allowed to lie fallow. The failure to use it more effectively restrains agricultural output.

Some *latifundios* have, however, become efficient cattle or wheat ranches or plantations producing sugarcane, coffee, and bananas for export, thus helping the particular country to earn foreign exchange.

Various authorities on the improvement of badly used land have made proposals, ranging from an increase in the land tax to the subdivision of large estates into efficient holdings to be transferred to independent farmers. The higher land tax would force the landowner to make better use of his land, while the division of the *latifundios* into independent holdings would stimulate production if it resulted in the development of an independent rural population. The independent farmer-owner has a direct incentive to make the land more productive because all the rewards of his efforts come to him, one important condition being that the holdings must be large enough to be economically viable, and at the same time, appropriate legislation must prevent their subdivision and fragmentation; but for the moment the landowners in most Latin American countries have enough political power to prevent such reforms. Land reforms in such countries as Mexico, Japan, and Taiwan have led to substantial increases in production because land was put in the hands of owner-cultivators, thus encouraging initiative, thrift, and long-term investment in the soil.

The story of the Japanese land reforms, however, is something of a special case. These reforms contributed to making Japanese agriculture the most efficient in Asia. In Japan as in other Asian countries the scarcity of land and the high rural density make for small-scale farming, with most of the work being done by members of the family.

When in 1867 the Meiji era began, the Japanese government embarked on a policy of modernization involving institutional reform, education, and technical development. In 1873 the feudal landlords (the *daimyo*) were dispossessed and the land was redistributed to those who cultivated it, that is, the former tenants. Holdings were generally small and hardly ever exceeded five acres. The new peasant proprietors now had to pay a fixed annual money tax of 3 percent of the value of the land, which meant that on average the peasant paid one-third of the harvest value as tax. This tax money provided 80 percent of the state's revenues. In this manner the farming community was made to finance the economic and social development of Japan. Harsh as the measure may seem at first sight, it did create the incentive for the farmer to cultivate the land with utmost care and to use the best technology to maximize output. He also learned to save and invest in tools and implements. Those who could not produce at sufficiently low cost could not pay the tax and either became tenants or were pushed off the land. Tenants enjoyed no form of government protection and were subject to high rents.

After World War II a period of almost seven years of American occupation followed. The Americans were determined to carry through a great number of reforms in order to make Japan viable, peaceful, and democratic. A rapid increase in tenancy had taken place between 1900 and 1940, and the new land reforms once again attempted to do away with the landlord class and transform tenants into owner-cultivators. The landlords themselves were not big landowners in the sense in which that term is understood in the Western countries. Their holdings were usually small, not exceeding ten acres.

Be that as it may, the Owner-Farmer Establishment Law of 1946 virtually expropriated the nonresident landowners. They could keep 2.45 acres in the three main islands. In Hokkaido they could retain 9.80 acres. Anything in excess of these lands was purchased by the government and resold to "eligible" farmers (usually former tenants). Ceilings were also set on the holdings of owner-cultivators. In the main islands the limit was set at 7.35 acres and in Hokkaido at 27.40

acres. These reforms did in fact transform Japan into a country of peasant proprietors. The ratio of tenanted land to the cultivated area declined from 46 percent to 8 percent.

Rents that before the war had ranged from 50 to 70 percent of the harvest were now also curtailed. Their ceilings were set at 25 percent of the harvest for irrigated and 15 percent for dry land. After the reforms the average-sized farm was about 2.5 acres, which is very small by American standards but may not be so bad in a very densely populated country where the maximization of yield per acre has become more important than the maximization of output per man-hour.

Another type of inefficient land distribution system is common in Western Europe, the Middle East, and Asia; as a result of population growth and the subdivision of holdings among heirs, farm plots have become too small to be worked efficiently. State-sponsored consolidation schemes, from compulsory swapping to massive programs of regional rationalization, are the order of the day in several countries, the problem sometimes solving itself. The larger and more efficient farm units compete the smaller ones out of existence, a particular farmer going off to the city while his land is incorporated into a larger productive unit. In many less affluent countries a rapid development toward large-scale mechanized farming is hardly desirable. When agricultural density is high and few new industries exist, the men driven from the farms would not be able to find jobs. This would confront the country with an unemployment problem that could hazard social peace.

Increases in Yields per Acre

Irrigation is a well-known and old method of increasing farmland output. Even the ancient civilizations in western Asia and Egypt relied on water control to improve their land. Today about 370 million acres are under irrigation in the world; it is estimated that this total can be doubled; most readily available water will then be used. But as stated earlier, irrigation is costly and the more obvious (i.e., cheapest) schemes have already been carried out. Present irrigation project costs are about $400 per additional acre. Reasonably cheap desalination is still impossible, and even if a breakthrough is achieved, there remain pumping, diversion, and distribution costs. Rain is the ultimate source of fresh water and therefore the limiting factor; in 15 percent of South America and Europe the annual rainfall is less than 20 inches (500 mm); the same holds in North America and Africa (50 percent), Australia (60 percent), and Asia (70 percent).

Streams and lakes and underground waters are replenished by runoff and percolated rainwater, that is, "controllable" water, though runoff is often less than supposed. In dry Australia, for example, only 10 to 20 percent of the rainwater received on the land surface can be stored and used. In the United States about 30 percent is runoff that can be captured.

Another problem is that all over the world industrial, urban, and agricultural competition for "controllable" water is sharpening. In such countries as the United States or France, industry consumes about half of all water used. Pollution of water by industry and municipal waste further diminishes its potential use by others; there is, however, limited scope for multiple use of water. Water that is used for hydroelectric power generation, for instance, is often available for reuse.

An additional problem with irrigation is that some rivers flow through several countries. This can result in great difficulties. At present, Ethiopia, for instance, is threatening both Egypt and the Sudan with its plans to restrict and divert the flow of the Nile.

A further undesirable side effect of irrigation is that it promotes bilharzia (schistosomiasis) in the rice-growing countries, where people cultivate flooded land barefoot. The disease, which is quite debilitating, is caused by a hookworm the larvae of which penetrate the skin of people standing in the water, and then settle in the blood vessels of intestines, lungs, or other organs; the eggs of these hookworms leave the body in the human excreta, develop in the water, and subsequently penetrate small snails in which they reach the larva stage. Once fully grown, they eat their way out of the snail and penetrate the human body, the worms and snails thriving in the man-made irrigation system—also used for elimination purposes. The disease now afflicts some 250 million people and is spreading. Additional irrigation works will facilitate the spread of this disease.

Fertilizers and Pesticides

The use of chemical fertilizers and chemical control of weeds have brought about spectacular increases in food production. Combined with a liberal water supply, the use of chemical fertilizers can triple or even quadruple product per unit of land. Farmers all over the world now use 60 million metric tons per year, which amounts to about 45 pounds per acre. Distribution is, however, very uneven. Japanese, West European, and American farmers employ them on a large scale. African, Latin American, and Asian farmers use much smaller quantities, if any.

Chemical fertilizers consist mostly of a mixture of nitrates, phosphates, and potash. Nitrogen can be processed from the air; but the process consumes large amounts of energy. Potash and phosphates are mined and thus nonrenewable; potash is fairly abundant, phosphates less so.

More and more chemicals will clearly be used to increase production, because population and incomes boost the demand for food whereas erosion and urban encroachment diminish land availabilities. In the United States each year the growth of towns, cities, and highways devours about one million acres.

Some observers have stated that the increased use of chemicals in agriculture may bring us an environmental catastrophe; and the first signs of the degradation due to these chemicals are with us today. The infiltration of nitrates into groundwater endangers the health of children and livestock; in some areas of California and Illinois, wellwater is now poisoned by nitrates. Inorganic phosphates and nitrates that run into lakes and rivers are as good nutrients to algae as to other plants. With the growth of algae the water is increasingly deprived of oxygen, the fish are killed, and finally the lake turns into a swamp. Lake Erie shows this process visibly under way. Phosphates from detergents and untreated municipal waste only make matters worse.

Since world consumption of commercial fertilizers is predicted to triple between now and the year 2000, it seems reasonable to expect a much higher level of environmental destruction in the future than we are witnessing now.

The pesticides, which are nearly all nondegradable, also create environmental hazards. Some 900 million pounds of them are used annually. While their use certainly increases agricultural production, these pollutants destroy other animal species and may also affect man's health. We know only too little about the effects on human metabolism of DDT and other chlorinated hydrocarbons. It is common knowledge now that in the United States concentrations of DDT in mothers' milk exceed the tolerance levels set by the Food and Drug Administration.

Even at this point a high tax on nitrate fertilizers and all harmful pesticides and fungicides is called for to prevent excessive accumulation of these pollutants in the biosphere. Taxes or laws limiting the use of nondegradable pesticides would encourage research into pesticides aimed at specific pests that are biodegradable and less toxic to man.

New Strains

One of the more interesting developments in agriculture, through genetics, has been the breeding of cereals and other plant species that produce higher yields and are less susceptible to disease and more resistant to cold or drought. New corn and sorghum hybrids have been developed to produce a more than twofold increase in production per acre. In the United States 30 bushels of corn were produced per acre in 1940; by 1967 the figure had risen to 80 bushels.

The Rockefeller and Ford Foundation scientists working in experimental agricultural institutes in the Philippines and Mexico have developed short-statured, stiff-strawed new strains of wheat and rice that mature in a relatively short period of time. One of the first "miracle" rices (I.R. 8) matured in only 120 days, as against 150 or 180 days for other varieties. Despite their drawbacks these new strains permit highly desirable increases in output. However, they require much larger doses of fertilizer, water, pesticides, and fungicides than the ordinary strains—which implies considerable investment in irrigation and fertilizers. In other words these "miracles" are very expensive. In the Philippines it has been estimated that growing costs per acre of "miracle" rice are about ten times those of older varieties. Only the more prosperous farmers can afford this; the new rice strains have failed in areas that are merely rain-fed and not irrigated (i.e., about 60 percent of all Asian riceland). Besides, the greater use of polluting commercial fertilizers creates environmental stresses.

The "green revolution" euphoria of the 1960s is now evaporating. People got carried away by the spectacular yields attained on the plots of experimental stations. The media and the public tended to regard what came of such research as solutions to the food problem, thus calming the citizenry's anxiety. The problem is that *record* yields achieved by the seed experimenters under special conditions cannot be translated into national or international *average* yields. The volume of resource inputs in research stations is many times greater than on the average farm. Besides, rainfall, temperature, soils, and managerial skills differ from farm to farm.

Nevertheless the new strains of corn, sorghum wheat, and rice have produced impressive yields per acre; but once the spectacular gains are achieved, chances of further increases wane. On about 95 percent of the corn acreage in the United States, hybrids have replaced the traditional variety, so there is little hope of the same annual increases in output as prevailed during the last two decades being sustained. Many agricultural experts, like Lester R. Brown, associated with the U.S. Department of Agriculture, believe that in Japan, Western Europe, and North America the upper limit of crop yield is being approached. Output, it seems, will still increase, but increments in production will become smaller and smaller. The law of diminishing returns reasserts itself. Research may produce even more productive hybrids than we now have; but no further yield spurt per acre beyond what we have known since 1940 is very likely. Growth in total production will continue, but growth rates are likely to slow down in the Western world.

A coming technological breakthrough bound, at least temporarily, to provide some relief is the development of wheat and rice varieties with a higher nutritional, especially protein, content. Complete protein contains 21 body-building amino acids. The human body needs these amino acids in certain combinations; if some are lacking in the daily diet, the others are useless even if consumed in large quantities. Grains such as wheat and rice are shy of lysine. Since many human beings rely mainly on cereals for their food supply, an improved amino acid composition would help these cereals to overcome the protein shortages so prevalent among marginally nourished people.

Greater Use of Farm Machinery

This is an expensive proposition quite out of the reach of most of the world's farmers. Machinery does not improve the fertility of the soil, but helps in various ways to increase its output. Power equipment quickens the processes of drainage, ditching, leveling, and terracing. Farm machinery can also greatly increase the yield per man-hour. In the relatively thinly populated areas of Canada and the Midwest and Plains states of the United States, mechanized equipment permits large-scale farming with high returns per labor input. Equipment also helps to reduce the number of man-hours needed to harvest a certain area and makes it possible to harvest at the right time. But machine equipment actually replaces human energy by machine energy and presently relies heavily on cheap supplies of fossil fuels. This quickens the pace at which these exhaustible fuels are consumed.

Other Ways of Increasing Food Production

The list of means of augmenting food production is far from ended. New plants that can produce food can be found. Existing plants can be introduced elsewhere. The sugar beet was only discovered in the nineteenth century. Potatoes spread from Latin America to North America and Europe. The protein-rich pea spread from Egypt to all continents. Plants sometimes do better in a new environment than in their traditional surroundings.

Through the applications of modern genetics we can find new strains of cereals that will grow in marginal or submarginal areas; at present a ninety-day corn variety is grown in the cooler part of Canada.

One major problem is how to encourage farmers in the less developed countries. They can only be made to produce more if prices are higher, and they should be allowed to keep the rewards of their efforts. Many politicians in the less developed countries rely on naïve development theories and believe too much in communal land use, cooperatives, and the like, or they exploit the peasant in one way or the other. In Senegal and Thailand, for instance, the governments hold the prices of groundnuts and rice at artificially low levels. The difference between the low price the farmer gets and the higher export price accrues to the government as a tax. In Senegal inefficient and often corrupt state-imposed cooperatives supply the peasants with fertilizers and tools. They are also the principal source of farm credit. When between 1960 and 1970 many peasants were unable to repay their loans, they were stripped of their property or beaten and imprisoned by the army. Especially the smaller farmers then understood the dangers of being indebted to government cooperatives and returned to subsistence farming. These are examples of how not to do

it. It seems much safer to rely on the good husbandman with the entrepreneurial approach, who should be made to invest in better seeds,
equipment, fertilizers, and improved irrigation. Only rising prices
and land tenure policies, which allow him to keep the fruits of his
efforts, will motivate him properly. A major problem here is that
domestic markets for agricultural products are often weak in the less
developed countries, where too few town and city dwellers have
adequate purchasing power.

In 1970 such countries as Thailand had exportable food surpluses
while part of their population went hungry. The economic history of
many European countries suggests that the development of the farming industry derives from the pull of urban markets. In England, for
instance, the expansion of new urban markets drew agriculture out of
its medieval doldrums. In a sense greater food supplies are behind the
whole process of economic growth; without the necessary purchasing
power, however, extra production will not come forth, while population growth remains itself a major obstacle to economic development
and increased per capita income.

The rural entrepreneur must invest in his land while often lacking
the funds to do so, and reliance on professional moneylenders is
dangerous because they often ask ruinously high interest rates.

One possible solution to the rural credit problem is the establishment of cooperative rural loan societies. Local people can deposit
their savings, which eligible farmers can borrow, while the members
of the cooperative can be bound to make a small contribution to the
working capital of the bank. This solution was tried in 1898 in Germany, where Frederick Raffeisen, *Burgomeister* of a group of small
villages in the Rhineland, took the initiative in establishing the first
loan society. The earliest banks were small and operated by honorary
officials, the only paid employee being the local priest or schoolmaster
who saw to the accounting. The "Raffeisen principle" has since
spread and been a success in other countries, one important condition for that success being governmental noninflationary policies;
inflation discourages the system by decimating the value of deposits
and loans.

Better education of the farmer is a further requirement for increased output per acre and per man-hour. He has to be instructed
in the proper use of equipment, fertilizers, and so on. All departments
of agriculture in the less developed countries would be well advised to

install pilot stations, training workshops, and the like. When Japan embarked on a policy of positive economic growth in the 1870s and 1880s, the government sent out veteran farmers and graduates of the newly established agricultural schools as intinerant teachers, with the task of instructing the peasants in optimum traditional farming techniques. That was in 1885, and the idea was a success. In 1893 the first regional research institutions and experimental stations were established.

The more developed countries can greatly help in strengthening the purchasing power of the less developed, particularly by abolishing quantitative restrictions and lowering their tariffs on their agricultural food products and raw materials (coffee, tea, jute, cotton, etc.). Tariffs might also be lowered on some of those countries' industrial products, and especially those easily manufactured in their light industries. The developed countries should modify their price support policies for their agricultural products, which have created large surpluses in the 1960s, possibly spelling ruin for farmers in the less developed countries. The drastic intervention of the American government in agriculture has artificially stimulated production, the results not being entirely absorbed by consumers in the United States or abroad; so the government gives the surpluses away or sells them on easy terms—which destroys the markets of overseas farmers.

The Communist countries of Eastern Europe could assist the less developed countries by opening their markets to tropical and subtropical produce, but have so far done very little to that end.

Seafood

At present the fisheries of the world provide about 3 percent of all countries' diets. So long as we do not pollute the oceans, possibilities remain of expanding fish reserves as foodstuffs. The present annual world catch of some 50 million tons can, according to reliable sources, be raised by about 50 percent, and thereafter yields would decline through overfishing.

One should not harbor too many illusions, however, about potential supplies from the oceans. First, each type of fish lives on another, usually a smaller one. The smallest live on marine plants, which need light, hence grow only in relatively rare shallow waters. Since World War II fisheries have been expanding, but the effects of overfishing are already becoming apparent; the whale is almost extinct, the harpoon gun, explosive charges, and sonar having severely shrunk the species, and overfishing in the North Sea has already reduced the catch of flatfish and herring.

The salmon in the northwest Pacific and the tuna off the California and Mexican coasts are also threatened. More and more countries are now sending out completely self-sufficient fishing fleets whose fishing operations cover vast areas and involve massive catches. Anchovies, pilchards, and other small fish are processed in factory ships and in plants ashore. The fish meal produced, containing about 65 percent protein, could, if deodorized and synthetically flavored, usefully supplement the cereal foods of malnourished people. Most of this nutritive food is at present not used for direct human consumption, but as fertilizer and feed for hogs and poultry in the developed countries. The effects of the increased small-fish catches are not known; but should the annual growth of 6 to 7 percent continue, depletion may not be far off.

Commercial fish farming also has its possibilities. In some Asian countries, like Indonesia, milkfish are cultivated in the brackish water near the seashore, living as they do as readily available algae. In Denmark alone there are about 1,000 trout farms, although the trout must be fed on freshly caught sea fish. Israel produces 56 percent of its annual fish production in some 12,500 acres of fish-farm reserves. Fish culture can certainly be expanded in many countries; what the significance of the resulting additions to the total world supplies will be remains to be seen.

Artificial Foods

All reliable authorities on artificial foods warn against fantasies and excessive faith in test tube shakers. As the prospect of universal hunger nears, people tend to escape their feelings of anxiety in the belief that somehow science will solve the problem.

There exists at present no large-scale commercial production of edible artificial foods. Although there are pilot projects in several countries, research still continues and even when new, safe, and palatable products are discovered, it remains to be seen whether they can be cheaply produced.

One possibility is the production of proteins from yeasts that multiply in the syrupy by-products from, *inter alia*, the sugar, wood pulp, and paper industries. It was discovered in 1958 that yeasts can also be cultivated on certain waste products of the oil industry, especially those with a high paraffin content. The proteins contained in these yeasts are accepted by the human body; but they are inferior to conventional animal protein. And the raw materials they are derived from, wood and oil, are by no means superabundant, as we are now beginning to understand. At all events, the harvests of these microorganisms can be washed and thereafter dried into powder or little chips that can be mixed with traditional foodstuffs such as soups, curries, bread, and biscuits.

Yeasts readily convert their intakes of feed, such as carbon, into protein; but economic and large-scale production remains difficult, although perhaps not insoluble.

Another difficulty is that social eating patterns will have to be changed if single-cell protein is going to have a significant impact on world nutrition. Market resistance to new foods is notoriously high, especially in traditional societies with a high percentage of uneducated people.

Summing Up

Gazing into the agricultural crystal ball is an uncertain business, says food expert L. R. Brown. Future output is hard to forecast. Many unforeseen events are bound to occur. We do know, however, that at present about one person in eight suffers from hunger and one in two from malnutrition. Growing populations and rising incomes will call for a doubling of food requirements every eighteen years or so—an unprecedented fact in history. The costs of the first doubling are estimated at about one trillion dollars. Can output be increased sufficiently to meet the growing demand? Land convertible to cropland is nearly all marginal or submarginal, much of it now being used as pasture; so more cropland means less good grazing land. Intensified use of land already cultivated may mean higher inputs and therefore higher costs per unit of output. Soaring prices will inevitably follow. Then there are the adverse environmental consequences. In base terms of "population effect," and assuming that it takes two acres to feed one human being, 140 million more acres of cropland would be needed to feed the annual increment of approximately 70 million people on existing standards. In reality we lose millions of acres annually because of urban encroachment and erosion. We may well be in a tighter fix than we realize. The well-known economist J. J. Spengler once said that the history of mankind has been little more than the history of hunger. The available evidence suggests that this is likely to remain so in the foreseeable future.

10

Population and raw materials

Après moi le déluge.

Louis XV

*To see clearly and yet not to despair, that my friend,
is what is fitting to our years.*

Stephan Zweig

Are Our Resources Vanishing?

It is a painful contemporary fact that mankind is facing ever-rising demands on the stock of depletable raw materials that lie buried in the earth's crust and are basic to the maintenance of our affluence. As populations and their gross national products increase exponentially (i.e., by a constant percentage of the whole over a constant period of time), the calls on reserves of nonrenewable raw materials become ever greater, the main points being that there are finite limits to the amounts of mineral resources in the earth and that in the long run the recoverable reserves will limit the standards of living attainable by a world population growing at compound rates.

Earlier writers have been quick to notice that no country can in the long term sustain an ever-rising consumption of resources. As early as 1865 the English economist Stanley Jevons, wrote in his *The Coal Question* that Britain was mining and consuming more and more coal every year, arguing that a continuation of the trend would entail the depletion within 110 years of all coal available down to a depth of

4,000 feet. Actually Britain "solved" the problem (1) by importing coal from abroad and (2) by turning to the new source of energy, oil, which could also be cheaply imported. In the nineteenth century the risks of resource exhaustion have been concealed by the constant opening up of new areas to European settlement and exploitation.

As with food, the consumption of raw materials depends on both population growth and economic expansion. But for reasons which need not concern us here, the population and income effects are hard to estimate. Taking the case of the United States alone, it is probably not far from the truth that an annual population growth of 1 percent and a real growth rate of about 5 percent in GNP (both typical for the 1960s) would result in a 3 percent annual increase in the demand for raw products. The dilemma of rising consumption of exhaustible raw materials has generated an interesting debate (summarized below) between the optimists and the pessimists.

The Optimists

Some of the optimists are economists who, it has been said, try too hard to avoid the "dismal science" label which nineteenth-century commentators pinned on them. Often they only consider the short run, up to thirty years or so. The argument runs somewhat as follows. Price movements usually mirror costs fairly accurately. If raw materials were indeed to become increasingly scarce, more and more labor and capital would have to be applied to extract a given amount of ore; mining costs would thus increase and prices would reflect the rising costs of mining poorer grades. But what have actual price trends revealed? In the United States the unit prices of raw materials relative to all other goods have not changed much since 1870. Even though poorer ores had to be mined, scientific advance and technological changes have produced enough cost-saving innovations to counterbalance the trend toward increasing costs. There is little reason to believe (so say the optimists) that in this respect the future will be very different from the past. The prophets of doom may argue that in the United States the relative costs of certain resources have not fallen because of increasing reliance on imports from abroad, while the optimists assert that rising imports do not necessarily imply exhaustion of domestic resources but simply mean that foreign raw materials are even cheaper than American. (In the late 1930s the United

States became a net importer of raw materials, having until then been a net exporter. Since World War II, the United States has become increasingly dependent on foreign supplies of oil, iron ore, copper, lead, zinc, chromium, and lumber.)

Some of the optimists also state that, if a country like the United States advances economically, its relative outlay on raw materials (i.e., proportionally to total expenditure) first falls and then levels off. The dollar value of raw materials consumed annually is something like 2 percent of the GNP, or a little less than $100 per person. This means that, if the worst comes to the worst, we could spend a great deal more on raw materials than we do now without really endangering our standard of living. As demand for raw materials continues to grow and high-grade ores become scarcer, ore and metal prices are bound to rise. This will make the mining and processing of poor-grade ores profitable. With higher prices the mining companies can afford more costly mining processes. The shift to lower grades need not, however, impoverish the country unduly because, as already stated, it can if really necessary absorb a somewhat greater outlay on resource inputs. And if any raw material eventually becomes exhausted, imports or appropriately directed technological changes may repair the gap.

The optimists also aver that each kind of input is somehow replaceable. As a raw material becomes scarcer and more expensive, substitution by a cheaper and more abundant one will become more relevant and profitable. Technological research will always find "substitutes"; lumber has to some extent been replaced by plastics and aluminum, while some cotton and wool fabrics have been supplanted by synthetic fibers. For certain purposes, especially in building, aluminum has taken the place of steel and iron. There are many other examples.

Developments in geological knowledge and research techniques will also find us new reserves of minerals and improve exploitation of those we know. The "continental shelves" (submerged geological continuations of continents), in particular, are beginning to be profitably "researched" and further exploration may reveal new deposits.

Lastly, the more optimistic writers assert that the slow approach of the future gives us time to maneuver and adjust. Since we will not suddenly jump into the year 2000 or 2020, given new information we can always change course.

Less Reassuring Views

The rosy views outlined above have been under attack, mainly from geologists and other scientists. These less optimistic writers say that mere concentration on the short run is somewhat shortsighted and unfair to future generations. While it may be argued that future generations have done little or nothing for those now living, a healthy society takes a lively interest in its posterity. The optimists, looking to the past, say that comparatively speaking, the prices of raw materials have not increased much, but forget that the future may well not be like the past. Generalizations about the future are rather risky, if based solely on a short span of Western or American experience. World population grows fast, and economic development goes on in many countries. If the 1972 world population of 3.7 billion lived by American standards, they would need 250 times as much tin, 200 times as much lead, 100 times as much copper, and 75 times as much iron. With the exception of iron and aluminum, known deposits could not meet such pressures.

Against the argument that greater imports need not suggest exhaustion of domestic resources, it may well be observed that there is little cheer in the thought that the United States's increasing reliance on imports is probably due to the fact that the cream of the richest resources has been skimmed off. The United States presently imports 75 percent of twenty different minerals it requires. In fact, few developed countries, with the possible exceptions of the USSR and Canada, have adequate resources to meet current demands; even fewer have sufficient reserves for the next century. Although dependence on imports of some essential metals is unavoidable given the uneven distribution of resources over the earth and international division of labor, such dependence does imply vulnerability. Where an unforeseen event like the rise to power of a hostile government in a country producing raw materials inhibits access to these materials, the welfare of the importing country is jeopardized, growing population and economy only increasing the vulnerability. In the year 2000 the present U.S. population of about 210 million people (1973) will have grown to between 271 and 322 million people, depending on whether two-child or three-child families prevail. By that time the GNP will have doubled or trebled. If even now this country depends heavily on imports of oil, iron, copper, lead, zinc, nickel, chromium, cobalt, tin, bauxite, asbestos, what can one expect the situation to be thirty years from now, and what about the decades thereafter? What can dependent nations do when countries rich in raw materials begin to restrict their exports? And this is already beginning to happen. In the month of November 1974, Canada announced that its daily exports of oil to the United States would be reduced by 100,000 barrels effective January 1, 1975. A total phasing-out of exports by 1982-1983 was predicted by the Canadian National Energy Board. A spine-chilling thought!

The optimists also stress that, at least in the United States, expenditure on resources is after all only a small part of GNP. So we can, they say, afford to spend more on them, as rising prices will encourage mining companies to mine deeper deposits at greater cost and speed up exploration. Small outlay on resources does not, however, eliminate the exhaustion problem. Some resources are absolutely vital to the economies of the industrialized or industrializing countries, and their depletion will endanger those countries' economies.

The oversimplified picture some economists and others have of a smooth transition from cheap high-quality ores to more expensive low-quality ores leaves out the truth that this applies only to a few bulk materials like iron and aluminum. Many critical materials have sharp concentration thresholds; so we cannot just move over to ores with a lower average content, assumed to become more abundant as prices rise. There are clear-cut breaks in the abundance of such substances as gold, silver, lead, zinc, mercury, tin, nickel, and tungsten. Besides, the simple picture of retreating to thinner and thinner concentrations of metal-bearing ores leaves out some unsolved problems of extractive metallurgy, such as the disposal of increasing quantities of slag, the need for higher capital investment, and the substantially greater amounts of energy required to process lower-grade ores.

The notion of replacing increasingly scarce materials by more abundant ones is again an oversimplification of reality, but one that comes easily to the economist's mind, since he is trained to think in terms of substitution. Price theory, for example, teaches that if the price of an item like, say, butter rises, the public will tend to replace it by another such as margarine, if the price of the latter remains constant. An increase in the price of coffee can stimulate the consumption of tea. In the sphere of raw materials, there are many examples of substitution, to some of which we have alluded earlier. The charcoal once used in the production of iron became short and was replaced by coal; coal itself has been partially supplanted by oil, steel by aluminum, and so on. The question arises whether some degree of "substitutability" exists for all raw materials. Some resources, like helium, mercury, and uranium, have unique properties. There is no certainty that substitutes for them will be found. In particular, the prospect of finding substitutes for the so-called mineral vitamins is remote. The public knows little about the elements essential to the alloying and fabrication of other substances; as in the case of real vitamins, the quantities needed are small, but their role is vital. Examples of such substances are tantalum, molybdenum, tungsten, and helium, some of which are found only in small quantities.

It is probably quite true that, as the optimists say, the continental shelves contain raw materials. The ocean floor itself is probably not a good place to look for new deposits, although some concentrations of nodules (mineral deposits that sit, rocklike, on the ocean floor) have been found here and there; prospects are probably better in the continental shelves. Mining technology for these areas (2.3 million square kilometers for the United States) is still in its infancy; but advances can be expected in knowledge and techniques. It is not known what exactly these shelves may or may not contain; but present prospects suggest that these areas will be a long time in meeting our ever-growing needs.

Some Facts

If population and income continue to grow in the future as in the past, the resulting demands on resources will be staggering. In the United States alone the demand for a number of substances might double or treble before the end of the century. Although it is a "renewable" resource, water is an interesting example. At present the United States consumes daily about ten times the 42-billion-gallon daily requirement of the year 1900. Should the three-child family prevail and GNP continue to grow approximately at present rates, water needs will mount to some 830 million gallons per day by the year 2000, which is about twice present requirements or twenty times the 1900 consumption. The maximum dependable flow for the United States is just under 800 billion gallons per day, assuming the execution, regardless of cost, of huge water storage projects. Reuse of industrial and municipal water will clearly become necessary, as well as desalination of seawater. Water will become much more expensive than it is now—quite probably up to 50 to 100 times dearer than now.

A world population growing at 2 percent per annum and a world GNP growing at 3 percent imply an ever-greater consumption of raw materials. How long will they last? Table 7 gives estimates of the survival of certain substances, on certain assumptions, namely, (1) that current world population and GNP will be maintained at present levels, (2) that no substantial discoveries of new deposits will be made, (3) that no submarginal deposits will be mined, and (4) that no allowance is made for deposits that may be found in the continental shelves—while ruling out recycling, and for the United States eliminating imports and exports. In other words, both demand and supply are underestimated.

The figures in the table, like those mentioned, are hardly conducive to cheerful feelings. As early as the year 2000 many recoverable reserves of such elements as gold, silver, platinum, tin, zinc, lead (and

Table 7. *Approximate Exhaustion Dates for Selected Raw Materials*
(United States and the World)

RAW MATERIALS	WORLD	U.S.A.
Iron	2350	2200
Manganese	2125	1967
Chromium	2525	1970
Nickel	2110	1970
Molybdenum	2075	2180
Tungsten	2010	1980
Cobalt	2120	1990
Copper	2020	1990
Lead	1984	1972
Zinc	1985	1980
Tin	1990	None in the U.S.
Aluminum	2125	1969
Gold	1985	1970
Silver	1990	1969
Platinum	1984	1969

Source: P. E. Cloud, "Realities of Mineral Distribution," in R. Revelle et al., eds., *The Survival Equation* (Boston: Houghton Mifflin, 1971), p. 190.

perhaps tungsten) will perhaps be depleted or close to exhaustion. Copper reserves will be scanty. Whatever the postponements allowed for in this situation, the days of vast unexploited natural resources are gone forever. The irreversible depletion of known mineral resources is proceeding rapidly, while the combination of rising populations and incomes will soon confront us with serious resource limitations.

What Next?

Although new discoveries may, and probably will, postpone the evil day, a relatively rapid depletion of many raw materials will have to depend on any existing submarginal grades of ore and scrap. It would, of course, be wise to prepare for the future while there is still time; but there should not be too many illusions about what *will* be done in the next five to ten years, because politicians here and elsewhere tend to think in terms of the next election rather than of the next generation. History provides only too many unfortunate examples of the politicians' shortsightedness, their specific qualifications being their ability to get elected or reelected.

The Short Run

One means of economizing on raw materials would seem to be consideration of taxes on those that are both fresh and near depletion, to encourage recycling, the search for substitutes, and economy in use. The precondition is to get rid of our "disposable, no-deposit, no-return, throw-away" mentality and to encourage recycling. The 34 million metric tons of municipal refuse annually incinerated in the United States contain large amounts of recoverable iron, zinc, copper, and tin. Every year 48 billion rustproof cans plus 36 billion non-degradable bottles are thrown away. We also dispose of 1 billion pounds of paper, only one-third of which is recycled. Of the 9 million cars, trucks, and busses discarded every year, only a small portion returns to the steel mills. While many of these "throw-aways" litter the fields, forests, beaches, and parks, recycling would make for not only a substantial saving in metals and other substances but also a lessening of the amount of waste with which our environment is burdened. Tax advantages such as special depreciation allowances to companies that install recycling equipment might encourage scrap recovery. Economists like Dr. A. Coale of Princeton University have suggested that a tax of ten cents per beer and soft-drink container would minimize the use of disposable cans, which are usually made of aluminum. Such a tax would make it cheaper for the beer and soft-drink industry to return to the returnable receptacles that, as many of us remember, were extensively used in the past.

We could also economize on materials and gasoline by driving smaller cars. To start with, a sharply graduated excise tax on weight or horsepower could be imposed—relatively low on light and low-powered cars but much higher on heavy, high-powered automobiles.

Another method of extending the life of raw materials would be to devise a special tax on short-lived commodities like domestic appliances and cars which would have to be eased as the products come to last longer. Many so-called durables now have a wasteful built-in obsolescence. A car now lasting seven years or topping 120,000 miles can easily be made to last twice that time or mileage. Appliances should be designed to last long and to be repaired easily.

The Long Run

Only a dolt would deny that a finite environment cannot sustain exponential growth of population and income for a very long time. Nationalists of all colors who love to see their populations grow will probably deny and perhaps ignore the fact; but the issue cannot be evaded much longer. We are actually already beginning to experience some of the limits to growth. Our morning newspaper bears witness. Stabilization of population and more responsible management of our depletable resources are our best hopes. In the end, our commitment to growth will turn out to be untenable; the sole remedies are a drastic reorientation toward stable populations and sparser use of raw materials.

11
Population and energy

An erg saved is an erg earned.
Kenneth E. Boulding

The usual sequence, of course, is disaster first, imagination later.
M. E. Sharpe

How to Create an Energy Problem

The best way to create an energy problem is to let your society operate on such implicit day-to-day "growth mania" assumptions as the following:

1. The greater the GNP the better. From half a trillion dollars around 1960, the GNP grew to $1 trillion in the early 1970s.
2. The bigger your population the better. The U.S. population grew from 100 million in 1918 to 200 million in 1970, and will reach 300 million between 1996 and 2021. In 1973 alone, 1,499,000 Americans were added to the total population.
3. The more big cars the better. In 1972 six million more vehicles were added to the existing car fleet, to make a total of 120 million cars. For every baby born, more than two cars roll off Detroit's assembly lines.
4. Consumption of electricity and other energy sources should be aggressively promoted, because the level of energy is an index of the strength of our industrial system, very much in

the same manner as an individual's bank account shows *his* strength.

5. Nonrenewable fuel resources can be squandered, because new technology will always replace them with new cheap substitutes once they are used up. Besides, we can always import cheaply from other countries.

6. Cities can be allowed to grow out instead of up, with the result that the average commuter spends annually a month of daylight hours driving to and from his job.

Growth in Demand

With 6 percent of the world's population, the United States consumes annually 47 percent of all global raw material supplies and one-third of the world's energy production. Around 1900 the United States used up about 10 quadrillion BTUs of energy a year. (A BTU or British Thermal Unit is the energy needed to lift a 100-pound load through approximately 8 feet.)

In 1972 the 209 million inhabitants of the United States with their 120 million cars and trucks, their 1,200 jet aircraft, their 12 million factory and office buildings, and their 70 million homes consumed about 70 quadrillion BTUs, a figure that is estimated to rise to 100 quadrillion by 1980. This energy was consumed in the form of 5.5 billion barrels of oil, 511 million tons of coal, 22 trillion cubic feet of natural gas, and 1,600 tons of fissionable uranium. The growth of population and the increase in per capita income, reflected in the expansion of transport facilities, physical capital, housing stock, and their appliances, have caused the consumption of energy to grow as fast as it did. A doubling of this consumption is expected to take place between 1972 and 1985.

The total energy consumption of the United States grew exponentially with a rate of about 5 percent per annum during the 1960s and early 1970s. Between 1873 and 1973 the American population increased fivefold while the energy consumption climbed seventeen-fold. In the next fifteen years (1973-1988) about 21 million additional households are anticipated. The car park is expected to grow by 50 percent and 40 million new drivers will be ready to take to the roads. Electricity consumption will probably double between 1970 and 1980 and quadruple between 1970 and 1990.

In the United Kingdom, for instance, per capita consumption of energy, which had been quite stable between 1900 and 1940, began to increase rapidly after World War II. The reasons were the same as in the United States: industrialization, more jets, cars, household appliances. Population grew too.

World consumption of energy now doubles every decade. If less developed countries were to reach the American standard of living of the early 1970s, world consumption of energy would be about 100 times the present figure. In fact, it will take them much longer to reach that level. Meanwhile, a tripling of present consumption by the year 2000 seems a reliable estimate.

Oil

The most important world energy source is oil. Twenty billion barrels were consumed in 1973. Recently other forms of energy have failed to meet their expected share of energy supplies. With a daily consumption of some 17 million barrels (or 6 billion per annum) in 1973, the U.S. energy balance in the early 1970s is as shown in Table 8. Table 9 gives some idea about the expected evolution of U.S. and world demand for crude oil between 1970 and 1985.

The sharp climb of crude oil consumption in the United States will have far-reaching effects on its dependence on foreign resources. In 1948 the United States was still a net exporter of petroleum; but in the early 1970s one-fifth of all crude oil consumed had to be imported, largely from Canada (25 percent), Nigeria (20 percent), Iran (20 percent), Indonesia (9 percent), Saudi Arabia (9 percent), and Algeria (5 percent). By 1980 around 50 percent of crude oil needs, or 12 million barrels a day, will have to come from abroad. The deficit in the balance of trade in fuels (the United States still exports coal), which is

Table 8. *Contribution to Total Energy Provision* (%)

Crude oil	39.6
Gas	35.6
Coal	20.1
Hydroelectric power	4.0
Nuclear power	0.6
Geothermal	0.1

Table 9. *Projected World Demand for Crude Oil (in Million Metric Tons), Based on 1973 Estimates*

AREA	1970	1985
United States	771	1,354
Western Europe	667	1,485
Japan	191	620
Eastern Europe, Soviet Union and China	340	1,000
Other	383	1,101
World	2,352	5,560

now (1974) just under $3 billion, may increase by 1985 to a figure between $20 and $30 billion. Since in the early 1970s the value of all goods and services exported amounted to $66 billion, the question arises how this country will be able to foot such a bill. Europe and Japan are in a much less favorable position because their domestic production covers only a very small percentage of their current domestic consumption. Japan's oil bill went up from $7 billion in 1973 to $21 billion in 1974, a situation that gave rise to a gloomy mood in political and business circles. The balance-of-payments deficit began to reach astronomic proportions in the United Kingdom in 1974. In Italy a balance-of-payments deficit of at least $8.5 billion had been predicted by the end of 1974. In 1974 a political crisis was added to the economic one because the Socialist party and the trade unions could not agree with the Christian Democrats on the contents of an austerity program needed to restore the balance of payments. Such countries as India are also put to severe test. In 1973, oil imports cost India up to $500 million. In 1974 this amount was expected at least to double, putting the country's balance of payments under severe strain. This is all the more so because the 9 million tons of reserve grains India possessed in 1972 have disappeared, and thus obliged this country to buy grains on the world market.

Existing and Potential Sources of Energy Supply

For the time being we will have to rely mainly on fossil fuels to meet our energy requirements. All fossil fuels are really based on solar energy absorbed and stored up chemically in organic matter (plants, trees, etc.) which has been buried under thick layers of mud, sand, lime over the last 500 million years. Deposited in oxygen-deficient environments that prevented complete decay and oxidation, these organic matters gave rise to fossil fuels.

As with other natural resources, the most evident fields that yield output at the lowest costs per unit are mined first. The less eligible ones come later, those more expensive to exploit. Presently most new American wells are drilled in territory not in the vicinity of the known fields.

Just after World War II twenty-six new "wildcat" wells had to be drilled in order to make one discovery of any significance. This number has now risen to a figure near seventy. The total amount of crude oil the United States will ever produce is estimated at 165 billion barrels. This included whatever may be found on the continential shelves. Some 136 billion barrels had already been discovered by 1965, and much of that has been consumed. The field at Alaska's Prudhoe Bay is small by comparison: 10 billion barrels. The total Alaskan supply is three to five times that amount. Without imports, U.S. domestic resources would last until about 1981. The peak of U.S. oil production was reached in 1970 with 9.64 million barrels a day, and we are now in the phase of decline, with 8.8 million barrels a day in 1974.

Various estimates exist of the amount of crude oil the world will ever produce, one giving a figure of 1,350 billion barrels. Much of that has already gone. About 562 billion barrels is the figure for "proved world reserves." The Middle East still has 352 billion barrels; other African countries, 53 billion barrels; Canada, the United States, and Mexico, 47 billion barrels; Latin America, 27 billion barrels; USSR and China, 57 billion barrels; Southeast Asia, 16 billion barrels; and Western Europe, 10 billion barrels.

The foregoing figures seem to indicate that neither the Alaskan oil fields nor the North Sea deposits will ever do more than satisfy a fraction of the total future oil demand of the United States and Western Europe. In 1985 the North Sea will only cover 15 percent of all European oil requirements, whereas with an annual American consumption of over 6 billion barrels (1973) the 30 to 50 billion barrels that Alaska will supply are little more than a substantial drop in the bucket.

Hard Problems Ahead, Even with Abundant Oil Reserves

Even should we not run out of oil, we would still have many problems. In the first place, areas where the oil is found and mined (on land and in the ocean) are exposed to oil spills; the tankers that transport the oil sometimes also produce oil spills. The areas where the oil is refined suffer from chemical smog. The cars, trucks, busses, jets and power plants that burn the refined gasoline products pollute the air with sulfur dioxide (produced by sulfur-containing oil and coal), waste hydrocarbons, carbon monoxide, and nitrogen dioxide. Sulfur dioxide attacks the cells lining the lungs' air passages and can result in respiratory diseases. Nitrogen dioxide is highly poisonous; it attacks the lung cells, tends to enlarge the blood vessels, and can in extreme cases cause a total accumulation of fluid in the lungs.

When electricity is generated, a portion of the heat produced is released as waste heat. The cooling water required by power plants is taken from inland bodies of water, many of which are beginning to approach their heat-absorption limits because the maximum temperature the various species living in those waters can tolerate is not high. In some cases power stations use wet cooling towers, small amounts of water being taken from lakes or rivers, and the waste heat being used to evaporate them. The problem here is that the water vapor released increases the local humidity and can produce fogs if the power plant is located in a valley. Dry cooling towers are probably preferable; but they demand larger capital investment and reduce the efficiency of the power station. The finding of suitable locations for hundreds of new power stations in the United States and thousands in the world is one of the many challenges to be faced in the near future. The electricity delivered to the consumer is converted into heat. Electric energy is used to turn on the lights, to heat the oven and the toaster, and to operate the air conditioner. In burning electricity and running their cars, the inhabitants of Los Angeles produce as much heat as 10 percent of that received from the sun. It has been estimated that if energy consumption continues to climb at present rates, the amount of heat generated by the population of Los Angeles will match that received from the sun in just about twenty-five years from now. The basin may then turn into a desert.

Foreign Oil

The increasing dependence on foreign oil which the United States, Western Europe, and Japan must face in the future will also create political problems. Most of the oil reserves are located in the Middle East, which is a potentially unstable region. Destructive competition among the importing countries for privileged access to oil supplies is just one possibility. When the oil crisis broke out, late in 1973, the oil-importing countries were unable to agree on a combined policy. If present trends continue, the Middle East production of oil will have to triple between 1973 and 1985. Will the Middle East countries be prepared to expand oil production to that extent? Some oil countries may be tempted to stretch the life of their resources and to stabilize if not reduce present production levels. Saudi Arabia especially, although still having vast reserves, has limited monetary needs and can hardly absorb the money flow it is getting at present. The year 1973 has also witnessed the increasing willingness of the Middle Eastern countries to use oil as a political weapon and to wring concessions of all sorts from the oil importers.

When in 1970 the buyer's market for crude oil became a seller's market, the oil producers began to act together and formed a producers' cartel named OPEC. The oil producers then began to tax oil heavily at the source. As a result oil prices quadrupled in 1974. Oil prices are now no longer determined by supply and demand on world markets but by agreements of producers among themselves. When the oil producers began to put heavy taxes on oil at the source, the oil companies passed them on. Professor M. A. Adelman, of MIT, has proposed that the oil-consuming nations remove the multinational oil companies from their present role as marketers of crude oil. This would oblige the oil-producing nations to market their own oil as best they can—which might perhaps restore a greater measure of competition. The price floor would then be the sum total of production costs, not the cost plus tax at the source as it is now.

William F. Buckley has proposed that a one-dollar tax be imposed for every dollar of export charge the cartel nations have added to what the price would have been under normal market conditions. Suppose a "normal" price of $5; suppose further that the exporting nation would put a $5 export duty on each barrel of crude oil. Then an importing country such as the United States should add another $5. The idea is to price the oil supplied by the cartel nations out of the market. Importers would be induced to look for the cheapest sources of oil while the cartel nations would have an incentive to break away from the cartel if they desire to maximize their revenues.

Still others, using the concept of "countervailing power" (restraints stemming from the other side of the market) have proposed that if the oil-producing countries have formed a producers' cartel, the oil consumers should also combine their efforts and act together in order to prevent the prices from rising too high and maintain the output of oil at levels acceptable to the oil importers. Here one could think of a large tax on exports of industrial commodities on which the oil-producing nations depend, or a counterembargo on all shipments to the oil producers in case of another embargo in oil exports. The years 1973 and 1974, however, have witnessed very little cooperation among the oil-consuming nations.

Shale Oil and Tar Sands

There are still very considerable reserves of oil-bearing material in sources that have not yet been commercially explored because of the high costs involved and the environmental damage that may result. Extraction of oil shale or tar sands requires high initial capital investment. Commercial exploitation was not attractive as long as relatively low oil prices (less than $6 a barrel) prevailed. Long lead times are required before commercial exploitation is possible; but now that the crunch is on, this source of energy is probably going to be exploited more intensively. The principal domestic deposits of oil shale in the United States are in Colorado, Utah, and Wyoming. Oil shale is a form of rock containing a waxlike material called kerogen. Under heat the kerogen yields an oil similar to petroleum crude oil. Some 55 billion barrels of oil are readily recoverable in these three states. For the world as a whole, the total of easily available supplies is estimated at 190 billion barrels. With new production techniques, more would be available. The ultimate resources of the United States have been estimated at at least 600 billion barrels. The federal government owns

70 to 80 percent of the oil shale lands and it has already started to lease out certain tracts.

The tar sands in Alberta, Canada, are estimated to contain about 300 billion barrels. One major problem with the extraction of oil from shale is that the shale must be treated in order to release the trapped oil; but this increases the volume of the shale by as much as 25 percent of its original volume, and the used materials must be stored or dumped somewhere.

Coal

The amount of coal consumed by the United States between 1860 and 1970 is estimated at 133 billion metric tons. Although the amount of coal consumed since 1940 is about equal to all coal consumed up to that year, the share of coal in the total U.S. energy input has declined relative to oil and natural gas. The mining and transport of oil and gas is less expensive than the mining and transport of coal. Besides, coal is an environmental villain, because the nitrogen oxide and sulphur dioxide it releases when burned heavily pollutes the air. Coal is still abundant in the United States, especially if compared with oil and gas reserves. Coal reserves are estimated at 400 billion tons, which could be mined with present techniques at acceptable cost. The ultimate reserves are even larger, perhaps about three times the figure mentioned. These reserves could supply the country with energy for several centuries. Now that oil prices are rising, the competitiveness of coal will increase, and higher consumption levels may be expected; but this will also result in more environmental deterioration. Strip mining defaces the landscape and tends to disrupt ecosystems that can take decades to recover. One generation gets the coal, but the next generation gets the burden of repairing the environment.

Gas

In the early 1970s, natural gas supplied around 34 percent of total energy in the United States; estimates show that there are still some 278.8 trillion cubic feet in the country. As time goes by, new gas wells will have to be drilled at greater depths and in deeper waters off shore. This means higher costs and therefore higher prices. It seems right now that domestic production will decline by a third during the next fifteen years.

American government policies on gas have been about as unintelligent as possible. Price controls have kept domestic gas prices artificially low. Consumption and waste have thus been encouraged, and investment in new ventures has been discouraged because of the low potential returns on gas production and sales. Considerable gas reserves exist in West Siberia, Algeria, and the Persian Gulf, although heavy investment in pipeline construction, environmental engineering, and overseas transport will be necessary if these resources are to be tapped. Many political problems will also have to be faced.

Hydroelectric Power

Hydroelectric power now accounts for about 10 percent of U.S. electric power supply, or 4 percent of the domestic primary energy supply. Experts agree that at least in the United States the most suitable sites have already been developed.

Nuclear Power

Nuclear energy seens a potent alternative to hydrocarbon fuels. Unfortunately it also has the capacity to unleash catastrophes that defy our imagination.

In 1973 nuclear power provided the United States with less than 1 percent of its total energy requirements. Twenty-nine nuclear plants are now operating, fifty-seven are under construction, and seventy-four more are planned. These plants are uranium 235 as their primary input. Energy is obtained by the fission process, which involves the splitting of nuclei of heavy elements such as uranium. The U-235 isotope represents only 1 percent of the world's total uranium deposits, and their supply could run out in as short a period as twenty to thirty years.

A transition to breeder reactors will probably take place before the end of the century. The breeder can use the more abundant U-238 (about 99 percent of all uranium deposits) and thorium 232. It transforms U-238 into plutonium 239, which is a fuel, and thorium 232 becomes uranium 233, also a fuel. A major problem with the breeder is that it produces waste that has to be stored for thousands of years in order to neutralize half its radioactivity. "Devoting all our resources to the breeder reactor is perhaps throwing all our rotten eggs in one basket," the famous economist Kenneth Boulding once said.

The fusion process seems much preferable to fission, because it involves fewer environmental problems and dangers. Fusion involves the combining of light nuclei such as deuterium and tritium. The deuterium-tritium reaction and the deuterium-deuterium reaction are the most promising. Tritium deposits are very small, and somewhat larger amounts can be made from lithium 6 and 7, both not very abundant either. Deuterium is found in seawater, and the supplies are large. Controlled fusion, however, is still a thing of the future. It involves scientific phenomena not yet adequately understood.

Nuclear power may bring headaches of unsuspected magnitude. As mentioned earlier, the fission process produces an assortment of radioactive waste products including strontium 90, cesium 137, and plutonium 239 that are among the most toxic and long-lived substances known. Strontium and cesium take about 600 years to decay to harmless levels. Plutonium is deemed dangerous for at least 250,000 years. The government has already accumulated 81 million gallons of waste but has no firm plan yet about what to do with these wastes.

Even now leakages are said to have occurred near Richland, Washington, in the storage facilities of the Atomic Energy Commission. Deadly radionuclides such as plutonium have been released. If they ever mixed with the groundwater, the water supplies of much of the Pacific Northwest would be in danger. We are now fully moving ahead with the construction of nuclear reactors without knowing how to dispose of the long-lived radioactive waste. Breeders are more hazardous than the present generation of reactors. A single breeder contains approximately a ton of plutonium 239, which is so toxic that if properly reduced and dispersed it would suffice to give lung cancer to every human being on earth.

Another problem is that of cooling. The emergency core-cooling system is supposed to supply the reactor with borated water should the primary cooling be lost through a rupture in the pipes. But the emergency core-cooling system, although it works on paper, has never been fully and extensively tested.

Some scientists fear that the pressure in the reactor core might prevent the emergency cooling water from entering should primary cooling water be lost. This could cause the reactor to melt. The concrete dome over the reactor would be damaged and deadly radiation released. The breeders are worse than the conventional reactors because they operate at higher temperatures. Earthquake, inundations, hurricanes, and other unforeseen natural events may wipe out all the safety features reactors possess. The danger of sabotage has been mentioned as an undesirable side effect of nuclear power generation. A small group of highly skilled terrorists could seize a nuclear plant near one of the big cities and demand incredible ransom or destroy the plant, so that radioactive materials would be released and thousands if not millions of people would be killed.

Energy from Tides

Tidal power can be harnessed by damming a bay or an estuary. The dam fills up with water at high tide and empties at low tide. But the number of potential sites is very limited indeed, and the initial investment needed is enormous. Reliable estimates state that tidal power will never supply more than a very small fraction of the total energy demanded.

Geothermal Power

Experts consider geothermal power as another minor source of energy like the tides. It involves the use of the steam or hot water obtained when groundwater hits bodies of hot rock in the earth. The "geysers" in northern California (Sonoma County) are now commercially exploited and have a limited potential for expansion. In the geologically active West of the United States, more can be done, perhaps with systems based on water injection.

WIND

Wind is one of the earliest sources of energy. The windmill appeared in Europe in the twelfth century and was used for grinding grain and pumping water. But then as now, areas where strong and steady winds prevail are few, which makes wind unreliable as a source of power.

ENERGY FROM TRASH

Another small but not to be neglected potential source of energy is stored in trash. With enough waste-energy conversion plants to handle the situation, the amount of trash yearly generated in the United States could yield the equivalent of 290 million barrels or

800,000 barrels a day of low-sulfur oil. The burning of trash may ultimately cover perhaps as much as 6 percent of America's electricity needs. At the moment eighty-eight waste energy plants are in operation around the world.

Solar Energy

Last but not least, the enormous magnitude of the solar radiation that reaches the earth is an inviting target. It is often thought of as a source with unlimited potential; but the fact is that it has so far been too expensive a proposition to merit much consideration. True as it may be that there are no fuel costs needed to run generating stations, the initial investment costs in equipment have been such that commercial exploitation has been out of the question until now. A great advantage of solar energy would be that it does not pollute air or water and that it avoids the environmental hazards of nuclear power stations.

The problem is to collect, store, and transmit the solar energy and to convert it into electricity; the experts feel that the problems are not insoluble. The favorable sites would be areas not more than 35° north or south of the equator. In the United States such regions can be found in the Southwest, where the cloudless deserts are ideal sites. The collection areas needed to capture the sun's energy would have to be large (between 23 and 70 square kilometers). One scheme consists in capturing the sunshine by means of specially coated collecting air-filled pipes heated to a temperature of 59° C. By means of a heat exchanger the heat energy would be stored in a thermal reservoir, to which a conventional steam electric power plant would be attached.

Some Policy Recommendations

The question remains what can be done apart from population control to avoid an energy crisis that would seriously damage our society. Normal market mechanisms should be allowed to operate. Price controls on natural gas in the United States have encouraged consumption and even waste while they discouraged exploration. Hence depletion was accelerated. The price system works well to make the best out of a given situation. If a given commodity or resource is in short supply, prices will rise and only the highest bidders—for example, those with the highest valuation for the commodity in question—will get it. Sparse use is thus encouraged. The price system, however, cannot be expected to perform the job of efficient long-term allocation of scarce natural resources. As soon as we discover how to use a given raw material and we know how to get it out of the ground and process it, that resource is usually gobbled up in a relatively short period of time. Once the peak production rate has passed, prices will begin to rise—slowly at first, faster later on. In the earlier period of the price rise, the response by users of the resource is weak because of the perception delay. Buyers do not know whether the price hike will be lasting. Even later, when prices rise faster, the users are enmeshed in industrial processes, fixed ways of living, and so on, which retard lower consumption. You *need* petroleum to make plastics, and if you live in the suburbs you will keep commuting even if the price of gas is ten cents higher than it used to be. Besides, at that stage of the game much, or perhaps even most, of the resource deposits have already been consumed. The peak production rate is over. In short, the price system tends not to give adequate and timely warnings when natural resources are getting near the depletion period.

Reduction of Energy Consumption

Looking at energy consumption from the demand side again, the question arises how can we moderate that demand. Compulsory programs such as allocations, rationing, and outright bans on energy use have immediate effects; but they are discriminatory and hard to live with, and they actually reflect the failure of government to act in time. As we are becoming increasingly aware of the fact that democratic governments have rather limited time horizons (the next election is more important than the next generation), we shall probably have to live with such compulsory programs in the future.

It would from every point of view be preferable to rely on a set of positive and negative incentives with regard to energy consumption. An example would be an increased tax on gasoline, which would raise its price and, other things being equal, reduce its consumption. But such a tax is regressive in the sense that it hits the low-income groups harder than the higher-income sections of the population. A tax penalty on high-horsepower or heavy cars would perhaps be preferable because only those who really want to drive around in a big gas-guzzler would pay it. We are certainly able to find a set of incentives and deterrents that would result in lower energy consumption if we set our minds to it. Cars have to become smaller and lighter. The average weight of automobiles can easily be cut from the current 4,500 pounds to, say, 2,900 pounds. The use of radial tires should be promoted because they reduce gas consumption by 5 to 10 percent. Cosmetic lighting can be brought down to lower levels. Better insulation of houses could cut energy requirements by 5 percent. The operating efficiency of stoves, freezers, refrigerators, and hot water heaters can easily be increased with presently known technology. Once we begin to think about it, there are ample possibilities of economizing on energy; but so long as energy was plentiful (and cheap), there was little incentive to do so.

Expansion of Energy Supplies

Private industry and government should consider special programs to speed up the development of traditional and new resources of energy. The government might reconsider its system of leasing out federal lands that contain oil or oil shale. At present, oil companies can submit a bid for a tract of oil or oil-shale land that is offered for lease. The tracts go to the highest bidder. This auction system tends to discriminate against the independent and smaller oil companies, which have the best record in the discovery of new deposits although their financial resources are relatively small. Many Western European countries lease these blocks out to companies or groups of companies that agree to spend specific sums on exploration and drilling in a given time period. On all oil produced a royalty must be paid. In this manner competition would be more lively and all oil companies would probably be motivated to greater activity. The drawback of this system is, however, that it could potentially result in discrimination and political favors.

It has also been argued that favors in terms of economic, technical, and even military aid should be given to such oil suppliers as have not used the oil as a political weapon (such as Indonesia, Iran, Venezuela). If, as now, the blackmailing countries receive favors while the others do not, extortion practices are encouraged.

12

Population and pollution

That which is common to the greatest number has the least care bestowed on it.
                                                            Aristotle

To discuss ecology without discussing people is theoretically possible, but practically it is nonsense.
                                                Judge W. O. Douglas

Our Soiled Surroundings

It is a fact that our environment is constantly deteriorating. Lakes and rivers that were once beautiful are now so contaminated that swimming and boating on them have become dangerous activities. In 1969 the Cuyahoga River burst into flames. Industries, cities, and municipalities transform surface waters into drains or sewers. Even now (1974) 40 percent of the sewage in the United States is released untreated. Some 30 to 35 percent receives what is called a one-stage treatment, which only takes out the solids, whereas about 25 percent receives a two-stage treatment.

In other industrial countries similar problems are encountered. The River Rhine, which runs through Switzerland, Germany, and the Netherlands, is so charged with concentrations of sodium chloride, arsenic, copper, cadmium, oil, and pesticides (which all reach the Atlantic Ocean) that mining of the river may perhaps some day become a profitable proposition.

The oceans are dying too. Many areas that were clear and full of aquatic life thirty years ago are now almost devoid of life. From July 1973 to July 1974 there has been an average of one blowout a month in the world's oceans as a result of the frantic search for new oil deposits. Between 1967 and 1971, nine supertankers were wrecked, releasing more than 2 million tons of oil. In 1974 twenty-six major tanker spills of 10,000 or more gallons occurred in the world's oceans. Larger and larger ships are being launched. Supertankers are extremely vulnerable because they are equipped only with single bottoms, single propellers, and single boilers. The ones presently produced are based partly on unproven technology. Every day, tankers discharge their oily bilge in the seas. At least 1.5 million tons of oil are annually introduced into the oceans. This figure is likely to become much greater in the future as we increasingly exploit the continental shelves and as the number of tankers and supertankers increases. By 1980 the continental shelves will perhaps produce about one-third of all the oil, and supertankers will be growing bigger all the time. (There exist plans for supertankers of 1 million tons.)

The dispersal of oil over the oceans may well imperil the supply of oxygen on which human life depends; a large fraction of our total oxygen supply, perhaps more than 50 percent, is generated by the oceans. The main producer is phytoplankton, the minute plant life that floats in the upper layers of the oceans, which, like other green plants such as the grasses that grow in the meadows, can capture radiant energy and transform it into stored chemical energy, converting the carbon dioxide in the ocean waters into carbohydrates through photosynthesis. Phytoplankton, in other words, uses sunlight to synthesize organic matter, releasing oxygen in the process. Photosynthesis can be curtailed by a film of oil floating on the surface of the oceans, acting like a filter and reducing the exposure to sunlight of the vegetable organisms living on or just beneath the surface.

The air is becoming increasingly laden with smoke, dust, and other pollutants, and breathing may soon become a hazardous activity at least in some areas.

The world's industries, cars, busses, trucks, and homes spew annually some 90 million metric tons of petroleum-based pollutants into the atmosphere, and babies now born in cities like New York have high concentrations of lead in their blood. Symptoms of lead poisoning are beginning to occur at a concentration of 60 micrograms per

100 milligrams of blood. A number of New York's schoolchildren have been found to have concentrations of 40 micrograms or more, while newborn babies in the Bronx (N.Y.) tested a few years ago had the same concentrations of lead in their blood as their mothers, that is, 20 to 30 micrograms.

The quantity of solid waste broadcast into the environment is enormous in a country like the United States. Industries are estimated to discharge 165 million tons of such waste annually, alongside some 20 million tons of paper, 36 billion bottles, and 48 billion cans discarded.

Pollution problems seem to have three basic characteristics. First, such problems accrue exponentially. In the United States, at least, the output of pollutants has been doubling approximately every ten years, which means that within forty years pollution can progress from a minor annoyance to a major environmental crisis. Second, pollution problems seem unpredictable. The deterioration of a river, a lake, or the air can go almost unnoticed for a long time until suddenly signs of breakdown appear. And finally, many pollution effects are irreversible, at least in the short run. If radioactive waste were ever to contaminate the groundwater of a certain area, it would take a long time, perhaps decades or more, to clean it up—if it could be done at all.

Causes of Pollution

A rising population implies growing pressure on the environment. More people mean more waste products. An "ecosystem" (defined as a series of interrelated cyclical events in which the life of any single organism becomes connected up with the life processes of a great number of others) may be able to accommodate a given number of people but can break down if that number is exceeded. Local crisis and even planetary disaster may occur if population keeps growing; population can act too as an accelerator of pollution problems.

The point here is that, because population growth itself can magnify the per capita injury to the environment (the total damage to the environment equals population times per capita damage), a 1 percent growth of population may cause more than a 1 percent impact on the surroundings. A few examples will serve to illustrate how this can happen. Should, for instance, population growth result in the

mining of poorer ores that take more energy to process, more polluting fossil fuel would have to be burned to generate the extra energy
needed, while that same mining of poorer ores also yields more and
more waste rock, which has to be dumped somewhere. Population increase typically results in attempts to raise food production. Where
the most eligible croplands are already fully used, either such lands
will be cultivated more intensively or low-quality lands will be taken
into cultivation. In both cases, greater amounts of polluting fertilizers, pesticides, and herbicides are likely to be used; or perhaps
irrigation systems will be built that will disrupt the natural landscape;
water may be pumped from a river or lake to the land most recently
taken into cultivation, any pumping operations being bound to consume energy.

The increase in per capita output and income is the second cause of
the pollution problem. The more we produce and consume per head,
the greater the per capita harm to the environment, because nearly all
production and consumption results in waste. As the saying goes,
"The affluent society breeds the effluent society." More environment-
preserving technologies can reduce the injury done by production and
consumption; but the harm can never be completely eliminated. After
1945 the Western world was characterized by a relatively fast growth
in national incomes and output, and the boom lasted with minor
slowdowns into the late 1960s. Rates of growth in GNP of 5 percent
were by no means uncommon, and per capita output grew in a number of cases by 2 to 4 percent. The upward movement of the Western
economies was enhanced by the Western governments' commitment
to maintain full employment and high rates of growth regardless of
the consequences involved, including the obvious accelerated
depletion and pollution.

Unregulated or ill-directed economic incentives are the third major
cause of pollution problems, in the sense that producers and consumers frequently shift part of the cost of production and consumption to others. The competitive process in our free-enterprise type
of economic system fails to distinguish between cost reduction and
cost shifting. Production costs to a firm's managers are the costs they
cannot avoid paying; if, for instance, a firm can pass part of its production costs on to the community by blowing smoke containing solid
particles into the air, it will do so, whereas a "socially well-behaved"
firm that installed pollution-control equipment such as "baghouses"

(which collect the solid particles of smoke) would have higher operating costs and therefore higher prices. Such a socially conscientious firm would soon lose its customers, because its products cost more than those of its polluting competitors, although the firm that pollutes and has the lowest operating costs is not really more efficient than the nonpolluting firm. Nor were the true costs of production to society reduced; some were simply shifted to the community, which then had to live in a debased environment. The general population then pays higher medical bills, higher laundry bills, and so on. Economists call this process of cost-shifting the externalizing of internal (private) costs.

In the Hawaiian Islands sugar mills used (until 1974) to dump their processed cane in the ocean. This is a good example of cost-shifting, because instead of taking on the costs of treating the waste, the sugar mills imposed a burden on the tourists and the fishermen and on all others who intended to use or enjoy the shores.

Farmers use chemical fertilizers to increase the output per acre; but neither they nor the buyers of food pay for the waste runoff in surface waters or the leaching of nitrates into the subterranean water supplies. It appears that 50 percent of the nitrates used in temperate-climate farming are not absorbed by the soil. The figure for tropical farming is 75 percent.

Even the car owner fails to pay all the costs involved in his driving; so long as there are no restrictions on doing so, he imposes a cost on others by disposing noxious gaseous wastes into the air. Our car driver has no incentive at all to install pollution-control devices in his automobile; if he did so, he would increase his driving costs, and if he alone controls his polluting exhaust emissions while others do not, the overall effect of his socially desirable behavior is strictly zero.

A fourth important cause of pollution is that less-polluting technologies and products have been replaced by more-polluting processes and commodities. This cause is related to the previous one, and the reason is often that producers and consumers are not made to pay the full costs of the environmental impact of their activities; so the new goods and new technologies were introduced with no regard to their spillover effects. Many examples of such technologies and commodities come to mind. Truck and air freight have replaced less-polluting railroad freight. But it takes 5.6 times more fuel to haul a ton of freight by truck than by railroad. Nonbiodegradable detergents have supplanted soap; synthetic fibers have taken the place of cotton and wool; tractors have replaced horses and, as previously stated, the land is made to produce more through the application of huge doses of fertilizers, pesticides, and herbicides; synthetic rubber replaces the natural equivalent, and nonreturnable bottles and throwaway cans make way for the disposables. This last example of substitution of a nonpolluting item by a polluting one is instructive. So long as containers were to be returned, the user of the produce— milk, beer, soft drinks—had to pay the costs, in terms of effort, of cleaning up the environment by returning the container. If he declined to do so, he had to forego the deposit made when the product was bought; but as soon as disposable glass bottles and cans were invented, the manufacturer offering this type of container removed the buyer's burden of cleaning up. Although the consumer of the product is now no longer faced with the inconvenience (cost) of cleaning up and returning the container, the cost of tidying up the environment remains. Others now bear that cost. Perhaps they are taxpayers, if professional cleaners are hired by local governments to clean up beaches and parks; perhaps it is simply the cost to the citizen of living in a littered environment. The example of the can and bottle also shows how the problem can be solved. A tax of, say, twenty cents or more on each disposable container would make it cheaper to return to the reusable bottles.

Industries and individuals are not the only polluters. Cities and municipalities also give evidence of inadequate "toilet training." They spew untreated or ill-treated waste into surface waters simply because it is the cheapest way out.

People may complain a lot about these things; but if they want to know who is to blame, they have only to look in the mirror. People continue to have large families in many countries; they favor or at least do not actively oppose immigration in others; they all insist on ever-rising incomes; they create markets for polluting products and become suspicious if the firm employing them has to install pollution-abatement equipment, fearing that it may result in a loss of jobs; they find it hard to pay more taxes to pay for better sewage-treatment facilities; and so on.

It is also true, however, that much can be done to diminish pollution, and if we are wise enough to stabilize our population, reduce our rate of growth of GNP, and adopt the right type of abatement policies, the outlook is by no means so bleak as our dirty, particle-laden air suggests.

Economic Principles of Pollution Abatement

Population stabilization is a necessary ingredient of any antipollution program; but it will not work by itself. Total elimination of pollution is neither necessary nor desirable. The environment can handle some waste. What is necessary is to reduce pollution to acceptable levels, which may differ from country to country. The engineer might be tempted to say that pollution should be reduced to any extent technology will allow. The economist would observe, however, that total elimination of any kind of pollution would be disastrously expensive for society; the guiding principle, he would suggest, is that we should aim at a level of pollution abatement that would maximize net gain. This optimum or appropriate level of pollution reduction occurs where the extra costs begin to exceed the additional benefits of further pollution decrease. The point here is that when the first dollars are spent on pollution control in an abatement program, the benefits largely exceed the sacrifices. Relatively simple, known, and inexpensive devices can yield pretty spectacular results. We can return to the returnable containers, use soap instead of detergents, drive smaller cars, and so on. But as we continue our abatement efforts, each increment of improvement becomes more expensive to obtain whereas the extra benefits derived from it decline. Society's welfare is maximized where the costs and the benefits of the last increment of pollution abatement become equal. Beyond that point the sacrifices of further pollution control would exceed the gains.

The second rule the economist would like to see adopted would be that the last dollar spent on the abatement of emissions from each source should yield equal benefit. If, in terms of better-quality air, more can be gained from spending a dollar on decreasing emissions from cars than from factories, we should spend more on the control of pollution from motor vehicles and less on pollution from factories. When the last dollar spent on control from all sources yields the same gain, balance is achieved and the benefits are maximized. This would be the case in a program to control air pollution if the last dollar spent on abatement of pollution from all sources (cars, power plants, industries, home heating, etc.) were to yield the same additional benefit to the community—in which case nothing could be gained by a further switch of expenditure from one source of pollution control to another.

Options Open to Policymakers

Although the foregoing principles are simple enough, the computation of costs and benefits of each increment of pollution abatement is an exceedingly difficult task. Rough estimates will have to be the rule rather than the exception. Some pollution-control agencies will do better than others. The various courses of action open to a pollution-control agency are the following.

Persuasion

One of the fundamental causes of pollution is the divergence between private and social costs. Firms only pay those costs of production they cannot possibly avoid, and they are forced by the competitive process to shift the avoidable costs to society. Persuasion is likely to be ineffective here, because firms wanting to clean up their own mess, hence to internalize the "externalities," would price themselves out of the market.

The same applies to individuals. True enough, some people clean up the mess they make, say, by taking their empty bottles and cans home after a day at the beach. Too many people, however, simply believe that they have a holy right to litter; so any appeals to them to behave socially are likely to fall in deaf ears.

Direct Regulation

Such policies involve bans, minimum pollution standards, and outright prohibition of polluting commodities and pollution emissions. Oregon has banned the sale of cans with detachable tabs. In 1969 the city of Chattanooga, Tennessee, simply ordered industries to diminish smoke pollution by a specific amount after a three-year period of grace . Furnaces of other nonresidential buildings also had to bring down smoke emissions. A system of operating permits and annual inspection enforces the regulations.

In August 1974 the Environmental Protection Agency ordered a halt to production of aldrin and dieldrin, two widely used pesticides. They are now suspected of causing cancer. Unfortunately these pesticides seem to have found their way into the body fat of many Americans.

In the same manner the federal authorities can set up minimum exhaust emission standards for vehicles with internal combustion engines in order to achieve a better air quality.

Whenever pollution is extremely dangerous, total prohibition may be the best solution.

Direct regulation is not without its problems: it demands regular inspections; program costs may exceed the benefits; and once a firm has complied with the regulations there is no incentive toward further reduction of exhaust emissions.

In the case of Chattanooga, where a lot of heavy industry is located, the program has been successful in drastically improving the air quality; but the costs of the waste-control equipment is borne by the industries themselves, which makes them less competitive on the national level. Identical industries operating in other areas with no or little regulation can produce at lower costs and thus capture a greater share of the market.

This shows that federal or national regulation is more equitable than local or regional controls.

Subsidies

This is not a very desirable method of pollution abatement. The scheme consists of subsidizing the polluter to encourage the installation of pollution-control devices. The problem here is that now the taxpayers pay part of the production costs that in fact producers and consumers should bear. The system fails in imposing on producer and consumer the full costs of producing and consuming certain commodities and actually forces the taxpayers to subsidize the production and consumption of products that are priced too low and therefore overconsumed.

Pollution Tax

This arrangement consists of a set of special taxes or fees that polluters must pay per unit of pollutant (pound of soot, ton of industrial waste, etc.) emitted into the environment. The tax should cover the costs the polluter imposes on society. In extreme cases of very dangerous materials, the tax can be stated in terms of days in jail rather than dollars, although outright prohibition is perhaps preferable. One does not fight murder by taxing it. Now the producers of pollution are practically forced to internalize the externalities, and market prices will again reflect all real costs of production. Those who call the tune are made to pay the fiddler. The production costs that were previously shifted to society now become unavoidable costs to the manufacturer, who is now faced with the option between buying and installing the waste-treatment equipment, and thus avoiding paying the fee, or continuing to pollute and paying the tax. In the latter case the government can use the fees thus collected to treat the waste itself.

People can also be forced to pay the full cost of their activities by a system of fees, which would enable nonreturnable bottles and cans to be taxed sufficiently high to cover the cost of collecting and processing the throwaways.

Car users can be made to pay fees on undesirable products. A possible example would be a tax on lead (in gasoline). The car user is thus forced to contribute to clean air maintenance. It would stimulate the demand for low-lead or no-lead gasoline, and the lead-containing fuels might ultimately disappear from the market because of their comparatively unattractive price.

If a heavy tax were thrown on the emission of such pollutants as nitrogen oxides, automobile factories would have an incentive to redesign their engines and offer cleaner cars. The "cleaner" cars would be more popular and cheaper than the "dirtier" ones and now the incentive would be corrected in a socially desirable direction. At this moment, however (1974), car manufacturers have very little incentive to produce "clean" engines.

Under this system as under others, a public control board has to establish acceptable pollution levels, and where these are not attained, the taxes or fees would have to be increased until they are. The system of taxation is more flexible than the system of direct controls and the outcome—that is, the reduction of pollution and the stimulation of research and rise of cleaner production techniques and more advanced abatement devices—is probably the same.

An important provision is that receipts from pollution taxes should not be spent on polluting commodities if the beneficial effects of the tax are not to be canceled out; governments should use such receipts to clean up the environment, and any surplus funds left should be spent on the provision of nonpolluting services such as family-planning clinics, education, improved prisons, and the like. The output menu of society will thus be changed at the expense of polluting activities toward environmentally sound goods and services.

Pollution "Rights"

Another idea now under debate among writers on the subject is that of the selling of pollution rights by an antipollution board. This idea, though close enough to the tax system, differs from it in that the antipollution board would determine how many harmful residuals the environment (the air, a river, a lake) can absorb per day, month, or year and would sell those rights at market prices. Suppose a lake can absorb without long-term damage 1,000 tons of raw effluents and, further, that, in the absence of pollution standards, the industries and municipalities around that lake emitted more than that amount. The antipollution board would lay down 1,000 tons of effluents as the maximum to be discharged. The industries and municipalities could then compete for 1,000 "rights" to release one ton of effluent into the lake or perhaps for 2,000 "rights" to release half a ton. Several options would then exist for a given firm. It would buy sufficient rights to release all its effluents, or if that was too expensive, it could buy some "rights" and treat the remainder of its pollutants, or it could treat all its residuals.

In any event, the lake would be protected, the revenues from the "rights" could be used to maintain environmental quality, and conservation groups could improve the purity of the lake even further by buying up some pollution "rights" and not using them.

We are not suggesting that this system involves fewer problems than the others; but once we really start trying out such methods with some imagination, the problems can be overcome.

International Aspects of Pollution Control

Effective pollution control requires in many cases national or federal action. If, for instance, pollution control is purely regional, industries that have to treat their waste have higher operating costs than industries in other areas where no pollution regulation exists. This would amount to an incentive for industries to move away from areas where antipollution regulations exist. Ultimately, then, legislators would have a choice between a clean environment combined with unemployment or foul surroundings with good employment opportunities. Such choices are hard to face.

Although global emission standards are still far off, they will become necessary too. The dirty air of German industries has sometimes reached Denmark and the Netherlands, just as the smoke from Detroit has crossed the Canadian border. Regional arrangements to preserve a lake or a sea are in the making or have been contemplated. The nations surrounding the Baltic Sea understood that it was in the interest of all concerned to protect it. The Mediterranean Sea is in danger too, and an agreement of all nations sharing its waters is in order.

The Organization for Economic Cooperation and Development, which includes all industrial nations, would be a good framework in which to set up agreements on pollution standards. The less developed nations will find it difficult to control their pollution too strictly because of the high extra costs involved; but once the advanced nations have made up their minds and shown their interest in the preservation of our environment, it will be easier for the less industrialized nations to follow suit. One could suppose, for instance, that when the more developed countries have agreed on emission control standards the less developed countries could possibly be asked to conform to the yardsticks adopted by the more developed countries only when a given industry has attained a stipulated share in international commerce.

The Ultimate Issue

In the short run much can be done to bring down pollution levels, provided that citizens and their legislators really seek this end. In the long run the battle will be lost if the number of sources of pollution (people and firms basically) keeps rising.

Until now we have been rather obsessed by an ideology of growth. Growth was always desirable, and the more of it the better. As Kenneth Boulding, an outstanding economist, has pointed out, such attitudes belong to the past. So long as there was still a frontier beyond which ample new supplies of raw materials could be found and over which millions of emigrants could flock, growth, with the concomitant exploitation and debasement of the environment, could perhaps be justified. The days of the "cowboy economy" (as Boulding terms it) are now behind us and we are now entering a phase of history where there is no frontier left. The earth is now closed and we shall have to live in the "planetary economy" with its finite reserves of raw materials. The pollutable reservoirs are limited as well. Under those circumstances simple maximization of GNP is outdated, because it is in practice equivalent to the maximization of resource depletion and pollution. It would be much more appropriate to relabel the GNP and call it "throughput" instead of output. Throughput, as Boulding points out, would then be considered as the annual cost of maintaining our population, society, and institutions. Like all other costs, we should minimize it and constantly ask ourselves where further economies are possible. A stable population would be a necessary ingredient of such a new attitude. That this new outlook is still far off is a fact; but it is equally a fact that if we fail to adopt it in time, our limited environment will confront us with far less desirable alternatives. This theme will be more amply developed in the next chapter.

13

The threat of planetary disaster

Seldom do those decisive forces, destiny and death, visit man without a warning. Before every visit they send an envoy bearing a message, so softly spoken that the words go unheeded by the recipient.

Stephan Zweig

Anyone who believes exponential growth can go on forever in a finite world is either a madman or an economist.

Kenneth Boulding

From Boom to Gloom

When the fascist powers were defeated in 1945, the door toward a better world seemed wide open. Once the reconstruction after war damage was completed, there was a great upsurge of confidence and faith in the future.

One of the dominant features in the Western nations became the prevalence of rapid economic growth. It became an accepted article of faith that prosperity would keep mounting and that it would spread from the more privileged to the less privileged countries. Economic expansion would facilitate the problem of income distribution within the relatively wealthy countries by making the poorer sections of their populations richer while making the wealthier sections richer too.

Growing prosperity would equally help to alleviate the aberrant poverty of the low-income countries.

Certain problems such as pollution did not go entirely unrecognized, but it was argued that new technological developments and growing material well-being would help to handle this problem as well. The prescription for nearly all socio-economic issues was more economic growth. Economic science was also greatly preoccupied with the phenomenon of growth. The ultimate consequences of economic progress were quietly disregarded.

Toward the end of the 1960s, doubts began to appear. Earlier in that decade Rachel Carson had pointed in her book *Silent Spring* to the gradual poisoning of the environment as a side effect of our attempts to increase agricultural output. Professor E. J. Mishan, in *The Costs of Economic Growth* (1967), developed the theme that we were deceiving ourselves by miscounting our national incomes. If we only subtracted all the real costs of economic growth from our gross natural product (such as the loss of human lives in traffic accidents and environmental decay), our prosperity might not be growing as much as mere GNP figures suggested.

A whole army of sociologists, demographers, and economists, like P. M. Hauser and J. J. Spengler, had claimed throughout the 1950s and 1960s that the rising world population spelled trouble.

In the early 1970s accelerating pollution, the quickening use of certain raw materials, and massive urban expansion suddenly raised the whole issue of economic and demographic growth.

From Gloom to Doom

In the late 1960s it became increasingly clear that, taking the very long-term view of history, the period of rapid economic and demographic growth that had characterized the last 200 years or so must be considered exceptional and even anomalous. It was preceded by and will certainly be followed by an age of greater stability because, even on the most favorable assumptions, present rates of growth cannot last very long. If a magnitude such as population grows year after year by the same percentage (say, 2 percent), the increase in absolute numbers grows all the time until it finally explodes. This is the essence of exponential growth. It leads to eventual doubling and redoubling.

The impossibility of sustained exponential growth was understood long ago. In the eighteenth century several writers, like the Italian economist Giammaria Ortes, had pointed out that if all obstacles were removed, population would grow geometrically (2, 4, 8, 16, 32, etc.) and that in the end we would all be packed like herrings in a barrel. The better-known British economist Thomas Robert Malthus also explained that, unless checked by some barrier, population would increase exponentially until stopped in the end by lack of land and consequent food shortages. The only way to avoid a mortality increase through such checks as famine and malnutrition, he concluded, was to reduce the number of births. In the nineteenth century at least, Malthus seemed belied by events. The development of the Western Hemisphere plus the astounding progress in transportation enormously enlarged the world's food supplies. But the nineteenth century was an unusual period in history. There are no land reserves left, and chances of augmenting food supplies are limited. It is becoming increasingly clear to all those who have studied the problem that we are running out of space and resources and that we are therefore moving from an era of abundant resources to one of much more meager supplies.

A recent attempt to come to grips with the new age we are moving into is *The Limits to Growth* (1972), a challenging explorative study that attempts so to arrange known data that they can be analyzed by the methods of computer-aided systems analysis. The work should be thought of as an exercise in global thinking that may point to some of the situations the present world dynamics may involve us in. The systems analysis method was chosen because it was thought that the customary intuitive approaches to problems fail when they have to deal with the complex interactions of human activity and the environment.

When *Limits* was published, it was well received by some but showered with scorn by others. One type of criticism was that there have always been doomsayers who had mostly been proved wrong by subsequent events. This, it was argued, was particularly true for Malthus.

It should be remembered, however, that the present situation is in many ways unique. The world population has never been so large and vulnerable as it is now; its growth rate has never been as high. We know little about the long-term consequences of innumerable synthetic compounds on man and his surroundings. Resources are consumed on a scale never before witnessed. The emission of waste has now reached such levels that it remains to be seen whether these levels can be raised much more without dramatic negative effects on human health and ecological systems. And the inertia of political leaders in dealing with these pressing issues is as great as ever. In each age some "dirty work" must be done to challenge widely accepted ideas and conclusions; furious criticism and sneering must be anticipated, especially when the new conclusions are alarming and prick instincts of self-preservation. *Limits* would seem to fall precisely into this category of action.

Short History of "Limits"

The Limits to Growth was sponsored by the Club of Rome, a rather informal organization of scientists, social scientists, humanists, educators, industrialists, and civil servants. It was founded in 1968 by Aurelio Peccei, an Italian businessman and economist.

It was the club's conviction that contemporary problems have grown to such intricate dimensions that existing traditional institutions and policies can no longer be expected to deal with them effectively. A better understanding of today's problems and the recognition of new, more effective policy proposals are the club's major aims.

In 1970 the club consulted Professor Jay Forrester (MIT), who explained the essence of his systems dynamics theories, whereupon Forrester and later his associate Dr. D. Meadows were commissioned to develop a simulation model of the entire world. The funds were provided by the Volkswagen Foundation. A simulation model involves the use of a model that reproduces a process acting through time and over space and shows how problems associated with the process can be solved. In the case of *Limits* a mathematical model representing real-world relationships was built and the computer was used to plot the curves mirroring the dynamics and evolution of the model under different hypotheses. Professor Forrester drew up the first model, and Dr. Meadows and his associates developed and amended it. (For this and other models, see figures 4-7 at the end of this chapter.)

Note on Forrester's Thoughts and Experiences

In our decision-making processes we all use some kind of a model, if a model is defined as a selected set of concepts and relationships that supposedly reflect the world around us. These mental "common-sense" models are often vague and incomplete, and we tend to change the underlying assumptions too easily, says Forrester.

In our endeavors to solve problems we are likely to fall into three traps when we rely exclusively on these instinctive models. First, our efforts to relieve one set of symptoms tend to produce new ones that are often worse. Suppose we have an energy crisis; how do a number of legislators react? They tell us that by suspending pollution controls and by embarking on an orgy of exploration, production, and imports we can go on as before. Result: the next energy crisis will be worse while at the same time pollution levels will also have risen. Actions that supposedly alleviate matters make things worse.

In the second place our policies derived from our mental models tend to relieve symptoms, not causes. When the highways get crowded, we build more; car sales increase, automobile production rises, and the new highways get crowded again; then we have to build more highways again. When house prices go up, we build low-income houses, which attract more people to our cities, so that we have to build more low-cost housing projects, etc., etc. Such solutions defeat their purpose because the causes are not removed, but merely symptoms relieved.

Third, there is too often a conflict between the short-term and the long-term implications of our nearsighted policies. Legislators, hurried and busy as they usually are, tend to prefer the short-term, quick-working answers. Such solutions can in some cases be reasonably satisfactory, but in others the day of reckoning is merely postponed. This running away from long-term threats is typical of much legislation. Next to the instances mentioned above, a classical example of such a situation not mentioned by Forrester is rent controls. When rents rise, governments have sometimes reacted by imposing rent controls. The real causes—too many people and/or too few houses—were ignored. What happens after controls are imposed is that rents become lower than they would have been without the controls. The demand for housing is now higher than it would otherwise have been, but because of relatively low rates of return on investment in housing, fewer and fewer housing units are built; so the long-term results completely defeat the legislators' intentions.

According to Forrester, we should carefully assess the strength and the shortcomings of both the human mind and the computer. The human mind is good at recognizing the separate elements of a social system and their causal interrelationships. The computer has a comparative advantage in calculating the simultaneous interaction of all the key variables over a period of time. Systems dynamics attempts to use properly conceived computer models that can incorporate known information and yet, because of their ability to interpret the behavior of social systems, they can come up with unexpected novel results.

Forrester applied his systems dynamics approach first to corporations that had such problems as a falling market share. In many cases it was found that the known and intended practices of the corporation itself, and not some outside factor, created the difficulties.

Forrester then turned the work on urban problems. Again he found that many of the solutions applied to problems actually made matters worse in the somewhat longer run.

Forrester next turned to the world and developed a model structure representing the fundamental global processes (1971). This model was called World 1. It analyzed the interaction of such variables as world population, natural resources, capital investment, world pollution, and the quality of life.

The various scenarios led to conclusions that are far from cheerful. Industrialization, it has been found, is perhaps disturbing the world ecology more than population growth. Ultimately it may lead to a decline of the industrial societies because of natural resource shortages or a pollution crisis that could wipe out part of the world's population. Agricultural production has until now grown faster than, or at least as fast as, numbers; but now there are few reserves of arable land remaining and pollution levels are rising because of the application of chemical fertilizers, insecticides, and the like. Population keeps growing until malnutrition and famine stop it. The resource basis of the earth is simply too small, and the capacity of the earth to handle waste too limited, to permit less developed countries the same standard of living as the more developed. In any event, industrial societies may not be sustainable either. Therefore the less developed countries may have better survival chances because they are still basically agricultural. They have less waste and pollution to cope with, and they do not depend so heavily on the world's shrinking resource basis.

Conclusions of World 1

Once the Club of Rome had decided to support the kind of research Forrester was immersed in, his assistant, Dr. Meadows, and his team developed the model and published the conclusions in a first report entitled *The Limits to Growth*. This report was written for a popular audience and explains the conclusions in relatively simple terms. The results of the various scenarios, each with modified basic assumptions, are truly disturbing.

The model includes five strategic and quantifiable variables—population, food production, industrial output, resource consumption, and pollution—and explores their trends and cross-impact over the time period from the year 1900 to 2100 A.D. These critical factors are interconnected. They interact on one another through so-called feedback loops, which can be positive or negative. A feedback loop exists when a modification in the weight of a variable causes the system to reinforce or to counteract that modification. A positive feedback loop intensifies and strengthens a change; a negative one runs counter to it. Population and births are an example of a positive feedback loop. Population increase produces more potential parents, hench more births, thus more population.

The growth of a nation's capital stock leads to more output and income. This leads to more savings, which, if absorbed by the economy, lead to more net investment, that is, investment over and above what is needed to replace wornout equipment, and thus more capital. There we have another *positive* feedback loop. Exponential growth takes place wherever dominant positive feedback loops prevail.

Establishing that in most nations exponential growth of population and industrialization prevails, *Limits* concludes that if current trends in population, industrial growth, agricultural output, pollution, and resource depletion are allowed to go on unchanged, our life-supporting surroundings may collapse within one hundred years, resulting in an uncontrollable decline in population and industrialization. The danger of present trends is not only that growth will gradually be brought to a halt by environmental constraints, but that because of the slowness of human, institutional, and environmental reactions to danger signals (delays in feedback loops), the carrying capacity of the earth will be partially destroyed, resulting in a catastrophic overshooting of safe limits. This would imply populations with nothing to eat and industries without ore deposits to process.

A second conclusion was that the more developed countries are now enjoying a high standard of living, a golden age, which is unlikely to last. The less developed countries have no chance whatsoever of coming anywhere near the per capita consumption levels in the Western nations. Moreover, technological change aimed at economizing in the use of depletable raw materials, the discovery of new resources, increases in agricultural output per acre, and the like really can do little more than postpone the smash-up unless such solutions are accompanied by a man-directed slowdown and ultimately a self-imposed cessation of growth.

Finally, the global model points to the fact that it is not impossible to identify a potentially durable condition of socioeconomic and ecological balance, which would entail a stationary world population and stationary capital stock, implying the disappearance of net investment. In such a condition basic human needs for food, shelter, clothing, education, and so forth might be covered while demands on depletable resources would be moderate enough to make them last far into the future. It remains a fact, however, that supplies of all exploitable and nonrenewable resources are restricted and declining, so that greater numbers inevitably imply a lower standard of living in the very long run. The basic dilemma in which we find ourselves is, therefore, that our only choice is either to curb growth ourselves or to let the natural system do it for us. In our limited environment, exponential growth cannot go on much longer. If we choose not to interfere, our disturbed and depleted environment will backfire, and untold human suffering will follow. If we deliberately elect to manage an orderly transition toward a stationary world system, the sooner we start the better the chances of success. A stationary state is the only available realistic long-term option. While it is not possible to stop population and capital growth abruptly, the very realization of the alternatives mankind faces is a good starting point.

The Meadows team has also identified some policy proposals that would effectively guide the transition from growth to stabilization. Under these, world population would have to be balanced by 1975; birthrates and death rates would have to be equal; by 1990 the world net investment rate would have to be zero so that the world's capital stock would also have attained a state of nongrowth. The makeup of the various gross national products (GNPs) would have to be shifted away from manufactured commodities toward the less polluting and less raw-materials-consuming services. Pollution-abatement policies, recycling policies, and measures to increase the durability of productive equipment should be accorded much greater priority than at present. Given the tremendous incidence of hunger and malnutrition in our world, food production should be increased and redistributed. At the same time soil conservation practices of the kind mentioned in our chapter on food should receive greater attention, especially in terms of the total investment devoted to it.

Observations and Comments on "Limits"

The general treatment of the subject seems reasonably unbiased and objective. The authors of *Limits* as well as their sponsors concede that the study is preliminary and imperfect and that much more detailed work remains to be done.

The study has been widely commented upon, particularly by economists. Some of the economists who in the past have endeavored to refine the theory of economic growth and who, therefore, may be supposed to have a vested interest in the subject have been especially critical. Most of their commentaries involved the following areas:

AGGREGATION

The model has a very high level of aggregation, which handicaps analysis. There is only one geographical unit—the world, with its one population—whereas the globe is in fact composed of nation-states with different GNPs, population densities, growth rates, institutions, and so on. Moreover, there is only one composite industrial output, which makes it difficult to distinguish between environmentally harmful and harmless forms of production. However, some modes of production are more polluting than others, whereas some industrial activities make much heavier demands on depletable resources than others. Had, for example, private transport been taxed much more heavily than public transport, a growing market would have been created for the latter; instead, we built highways and thus encouraged high-energy-consuming and highly polluting private transport. In both cases transportation grew; but through our actions we turned the quality and composition of the growth away from the more economical and cleaner types of growth. There is in *Limits* only one nonrenewable resource and one pollutant. In an aggregate model of this kind either the world collapses, say from a pollution disaster, or nothing happens. In reality pollution disasters tend to be local. A river gets poisoned, a lake dies, smog hangs over a city, and so on. It seems that in the future more local pollution disasters will occur. Such disasters need not be worldwide. The same applies to population. Famines and population reductions will certainly occur in the future and are in fact taking place now. But famines are local and are likely to remain so in the future.

With no distinction between the various nonrenewable resources, there will be "business as usual" or a worldwide depletion of those resources. Again, in the real world, local supply "inelasticities" (scarcities) of certain distinct raw materials are likely to become increasingly frequent, as we noticed in our discussion on resources. It need not be a sudden, worldwide exhaustion of all resources.

But *Limits*, we should remember, did not claim to be more than a pilot study. Subsequently more local and detailed research efforts will, it is to be hoped, demonstrate to what extent the high level of aggregation made the conclusions inaccurate. There is right now not much reason to believe that less aggregative models would yield much more comforting conclusions.

POPULATION

Limits seems to assume that mortality and fertility levels are largely determined by economic conditions such as output and income. For example, incomes rise, health improves, mortality declines, population increases. This is true, but it ceases to be so beyond the point when no further gains in mortality reduction are possible. The Meadows team also seems to postulate that a successful birth control campaign through a reduction of births would increase per capita income, which would reduce deaths and thus set off a new population upsurge. It seems rather that there are no iron relationships among income, output, and population. Many other factors intervene. Strong population policies, family planning programs, changing attitudes toward family, marriage, and sex, the availability of new contraceptives, new laws on abortion, and so forth—all seem to modify the form and quantitative importance of the known historical relationships.

RESOURCES

It was mentioned in our section on aggregation that *Limits* treats all natural nonrenewable resources as one. Scarcities (technically called "supply inelasticities") will then afflict all resources at the same time. In reality, of course, specific resources will become scarce, others will disappear, and still others will be discovered. The Bureau of the Mines warns that 80 percent of the data about natural resources it provides have a confidence level of less than 65 percent. The authors of *Limits* who used these data are well aware of this and assume an increase in resource reserves by a factor of five. This estimate may be too pessimistic or too optimistic; there is at the moment no way of knowing. If it is too pessimistic—if, for instance, our known resource reserves can be increased by a factor of ten or more—we shall have more breathing space, although this would not extricate us from the problem of exponential growth. Resource reserves by a factor of more than five would provide us with more time for adjustment and maneuvering.

We can also expect some help from the kind of adjustment mechanisms such as prices that have operated in the past with a fair amount of effectiveness. If raw products become scarce and their prices therefore rise, and incentive is created to reduce the resource content of certain goods, lighter cars will be produced. We should add here, however, that several scenarios in the model assumed a reduction of resource inputs (for equal output) by a factor of four. Rising resource prices will also provoke a shift to more abundant substitutes insofar as they exist. An aluminum desk is not necessarily preferable to a wooden one (I prefer a wooden one), but it helps to save scarce wood. Just as we shifted from coal to oil and natural gas, we will have to shift to oil shale, of which the United States has fairly abundant deposits. This resource substitution is not without its problems; and it will not rescue us forever from the problems associated with accelerating industrial and population growth, although it extends the period of grace and gives us time to come up with any adaptive policies we are creative enough to produce. Recycling will possibly also be encouraged by rising resource prices. Resourcefulness, in short, although not a substitute for new physical natural resources, will help to slow down the rate of decline, if decline is inevitable. Present policies, however, do not show much skill; price controls on natural gas have encouraged wasteful consumption, whereas the maintenance of special low freight rates for lumber and minerals discourages recycling.

Rising resource prices will also help to slow down industrialization rates, because raw materials are a cost to industry, and other things being equal, rising costs reduce profit margins and therefore make investment and expansion less attractive. Taxing pollutive activities would have the same effect. It implies that we now force enterprises to internalize costs that previously were passed on to the community. Another proposal that probably would have a negative effect on net investment, and which would force producer and consumer to pay the full costs of resource depletion, is a tax on raw materials. Producers and consumers have, until recently, paid only costs of extracting, processing, and transporting the raw materials. But this system fails to account for exhaustion. A properly conceived resource tax would oblige producer and consumer to pay the full costs of using finite resources.

TECHNOLOGY

The model presented in *Limits* has not treated technology as growing exponentially. On the contrary, although it is assumed that technology will continue to advance, it is equally postulated that technology is not immune from diminishing returns. This implies, it is argued, that the most obvious inventions are made first; later further technological advances can only be made at the cost of ever-growing effort and investment. Since we shall probably also be forced to devote increasing research efforts to rectifying the side effects of economic and demographic growth, the net results of technological advance in terms of increased output are likely to become smaller and smaller. We also have to face the problem of institutional reluctance to apply the discoveries already made. Governmental institutions and corporations are not always eager to adopt feasible technologies, especially when this implies painful adjustments. Municipal waste can be adequately treated with existing technologies; but too often this is not done.

The model presented in *Limits* only incorporates feasible and institutionalized technologies. Technologies that are practicable but not institutionalized (such as the harnessing of solar energy) and technological discoveries that have not, or not yet, been made are not part of the model. Although this is possibly the only realistic way to treat the subject, it implies that the future may be very different from what *Limits* suggests if institutional resistance to the adoption of feasible technologies diminishes and/or if entirely new and unexpected discoveries are made. Although it is unwise to put excessive faith in testtube shakers, new findings will probably come across. As to the speed and magnitude of those future findings, we can merely guess, and no estimate should be taken too seriously.

POLLUTION

Limits asserts that with continued economic growth the pollution buildup may become such that world collapse will become unavoidable. It was already mentioned that the model considered only one pollutant, which decomposes very slowly. The model further assumes that the world can absorb four times the present annual level of pollutants broadcast into the environment. It is admitted by Dr. Aurelio Peccei that this was merely the best available educated guess. Little is known about the amount of pollution the world can absorb; it may be greater or smaller than the above-mentioned guess. The model further surmises that pollution will grow proportionally to the amount of productive capital equipment per head. The model has to do this because, as we saw in the preceding section, pollution abatement technologies that are not institutionalized and those that are not invented were left out. Since at present (1974) very little is done in this direction, *Limits* had to make the above-mentioned assumption. It goes without saying of course that the flow of pollutants can be impressively reduced if proper measures are taken; but this would imply that the present inertia of legislators had somehow been overcome. If this were to take place, there could be more industrialization with little extra pollution. The World Bank has calculated that such a dramatic reduction in pollution could be bought in the United States at the price of $16 billion a year, which is about one-third of the annual increase in the 1971 gross national product.

The authors of *Limits* knew that pollution could be drastically brought down. When this assumption was incorporated in their scenarios, it was estimated that pollution could at best be reduced by 75 percent. This figure was attained by calculating what existing abatement techniques could achieve if they were institutionalized. This estimate seems somewhat low, and since the model can only work with feasible and known data, possible future discoveries have to be disregarded. But this adds another element of uncertainty to the future world pictures drawn by *Limits*.

Last Thoughts on Limits

Prophecies can be self-fulfilling when ignored; if we listen and act in time, they tend to be self-defeating. *Limits* was certainly not ignored and therefore there is perhaps some hope that as a prophecy it will fall in the second category. Now for a few final considerations.

One assumption which underlies the entire endeavor of *Limits* is that there will be no major wars, which are heavy polluters, consume enormous amounts of raw materials, and are destructive of physical capital. This is of course quite an assumption; in the present century alone we have had two major world wars and dozens of small ones. (The most recent ones in Cyprus, in the Middle East, in Vietnam, and that between India and Pakistan, have all taken place in the less developed countries.) Technology is spreading, and extremely potent weapons are becoming available to almost every nation. The "merchants of death," that is, the major suppliers of the deadly toys (United States, USSR, France, and United Kingdom), seem to see to it that everyone gets his share. One can only hope that crowded and dissatisfied nations often ruled by ambitious generals will not use these gruesome playthings. Realistically, the possibility of more local and even worldwide conflagration simply cannot be lightly discarded.

It is especially distressing to note that the world now spends annually (1973 figure calculated at 1972 prices) $241 billion on armaments. The United States spends almost $80 billion per year, although this figure has not risen during the last few years. The armament spending in the USSR is also quite stable. In the less developed countries, however, the figures of defense spending are sharply rising. Needless to say, this is a heavy millstone around the neck of the human race. Compared to the annual $241 billion armaments bill, the aid figures look very modest. In the early 1970s, the annual aid flow from developed to less developed countries amounted to about $9 billion, including the aid given by international agencies. Added to this was an annual flow of private capital of about $7 to $8 billion. One cannot help wondering what a good investment in peace it would be if fewer resources were devoted to defense and more to development.

Presently most of the more developed countries find it difficult to give more than 1 percent of their GNP as official assistance to the less developed, and many countries, like the United States, give considerably less than that percentage. The authors of *Limits* conclude that by 1990 the world's capital stock should be stabilized and economic growth should come to an end if we want to avoid collapse in the twenty-first century. Average per capita income for all world inhabitants would somehow be fixed at $1,800. This would of course imply a massive redistribution of income; but how that could be done is difficult to see in a world where even national assistance amounting to less than 1 percent of GNP is under heavy fire. The rising prices of raw materials and oil, however, will help to redistribute income away from the resource-importing developed countries to the benefit of those less developed countries that export resources.

Another fact not to be forgotten is that an economic system that has achieved zero growth is not necessarily a clean one; a society can be stationary and polluted. It therefore seems to us that it is more important to think in terms of nonpolluting growth than in terms of no growth at all. The more developed countries especially need more long-term economic growth to rise above present poverty levels; but it is highly desirable that the kind of measures described in our chapter on pollution should be taken as soon as possible in order to avoid environmentally destructive growth. Another priority measure is population control. The countries in the temperate zone are now coming close to zero population growth, but most Asian, African, and Latin American countries are still far removed from that ideal. Those countries that are characterized by real or disguised unemployment would actually greatly benefit by a declining population. The total output of the nation would not suffer, but it would be shared among a diminishing number of people. Per capita incomes could thus rise even without positive economic growth. How zero or negative population growth can possibly be achieved is described in the policy chapter of this book. The major obstacle to pollution control and population control, it seems to us, is neither the technology nor the financial side of it, but the general inertia of human beings and their legislators, their constant preoccupation with immediate problems, and their general indifference toward coming generations.

LIMITS TO GROWTH MODELS

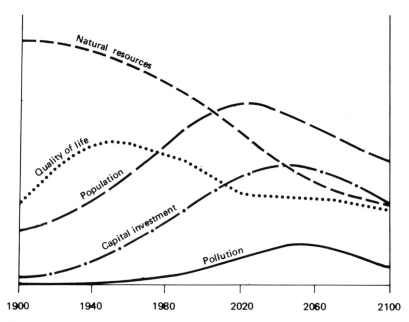

*Figure 4. Forrester's basic model. Declining natural resources stop the growth of pop-
ulation and industrialization.*

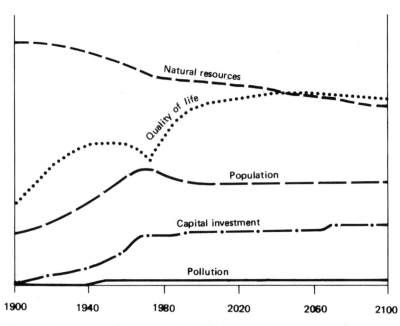

Figure 5. Forrester's equilibrium model. In 1970 the rate of capital accumulation is reduced by 40 percent, the birth rate by 50 percent, pollution generation is cut in half, food production is reduced by 20 percent, and the consumption of exhaustible raw materials is reduced by 75 percent.

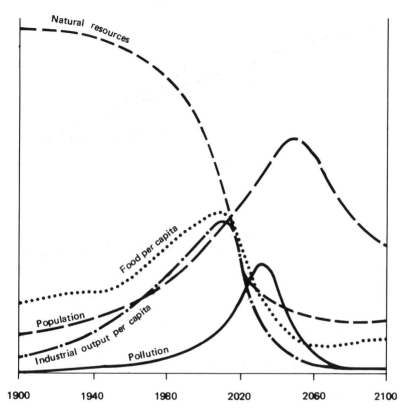

Figure 6. The world standard run as shown in The Limits to Growth. *No major change in present rates of population growth, investment, food production, resource use, and pollution is assumed. The result is overshoot and collapse before the year 2100. Taken and adapted from* The Limits to Growth: A Report for The Club of Rome's Project on the Predicament of Mankind, *by Donella H. Meadows, Dennis L. Meadows, Jorgen Randers, William W. Behrens III. A Potomac Associates book published by Universe Books, New York, 1972. Graphics by Potomac Associates.*

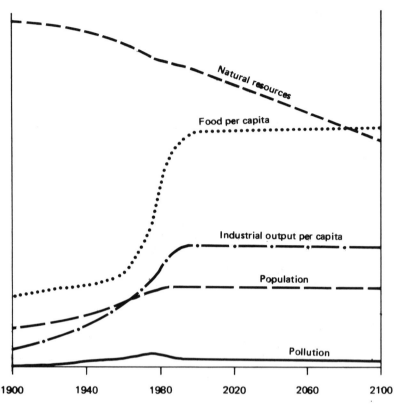

Figure 7. The stabilized world model of Limits. Birthrates and death rates are equalized by 1975; productive equipment is allowed to increase until 1990 and thereafter only replacement investment occurs; in 1975 resource input per unit of manufactured product is reduced to 25 percent of its 1970 value; the output menu is revised and becomes more and more oriented toward the nonpolluting services; in 1975 the output of pollutants is reduced to 25 percent of 1970 levels; more is invested in food production but also in soil conservation practices; tools and equipment will be designed to last much longer than at present. The model now shows levels of population and economic development that are sustainable over a very long period of time. Taken and adapted from The Limits to Growth: A Report for The Club of Rome's Project on the Predicament of Mankind, *by Donella H. Meadows, Dennis L. Meadows, Jorgen Randers, William W. Behrens III. A Potomac Associates book published by Universe Books, New York, 1972. Graphics by Potomac Associates.*

14

Should low-income countries with high fertility qualify for aid?

> *The question of population raises so much emotion and touches such deeply buried complexes that logic plays very little part in the discussion.*
>
> Joan Robinson

Two Questions

Statistics leave in no doubt the fact that fertility is highest in the low-income countries, that is, those that are most in need of the various existing forms of "aid." Two questions on the subject have been raised in recent years: (1) Should countries like the United States with a food surplus give food aid to all applicants, or should some sort of selection be made? (2) Should grants, loans, and credits be given to all less developed countries, or only to those showing willingness to help themselves by energetic population control programs? Until recently there was no relationship between aid given and population growth and/or density.

Food Aid

There are few countries now left with sizable food surpluses. Canada and Australia do produce food in excess of domestic needs; but the only country in a position to give away sizable quantities of grain foods is the United States. The daily world population increase of about 200,000 (or some 73 million per year) is bound at some time in the future to outstrip increased food production. The widening hunger gap raises the questions to whom and to what extent should the United States give food aid. In the early 1960s, a time of large food surpluses, some 90 million tons of grains were annually traded on world markets, whereas the Western nations gave some 10 million tons away. By the end of the century the less developed countries will be short by about 150 million tons per year, so that, even if the West (and the United States in particular) attained its full agricultural potential and gave away about five times the previous 10 million tons (about the possible maximum amount), still only one-third of needs would be covered.

The surging population explosion seems to promise rising food prices in the future, with more and more countries becoming dependent on charity. Professor P. R. Ehrlich of Stanford University, author of such works as *The Population Bomb* and *Population, Resources, Environment*, has proposed that the United States should now announce its intention to give no more food aid to any low-income/high-fertility country unless the latter demonstrates its self-help sincerely by initiating a large-scale birth control program. Second, the United States should no longer supply food aid to countries where the food population imbalance is beyond repair. The flow of aid in the form of family-planning technology and devices to all interested countries could then be increased, as well as the flow of technical assistance in agriculture to all asking for it.

Another imaginative proposal has been made by the brothers William and Paul Paddock, the authors of *Famine—1975*. As the food and population situation grows worse, the United States should, they say, consider a method whereby its limited food surpluses could save a maximum number of lives. According to these writers, the optimum solution would lie in a system of "triage," a term borrowed from military medicine. When the flow of casualties near a battlefield becomes too big for the medical staff to handle, a selection has to be made of who is going to get medical care and who is not. An optimal system of "triage" saves the greatest number of lives with the limited medical resources available. The wounded are classified in three categories: (1) those so badly wounded that they will die regardless of medical treatment, (2) those who can survive without immediate medical care, and (3) those who can only be saved if immediate care is given. Only the last category qualifies for treatment.

Nations applying for food aid might be classified in a similar manner. Countries where birthrates are out of control and likely to remain so for a long time to come, and which have reached an irreversible state of food/population imbalance, should not qualify for food aid. This is especially true if a population policy and family-planning programs are nonexistent or ineffective, and where leadership is inadequate and not committed to imaginative programs to reduce fertility and to increase agricultural output. Food shipments might provide some temporary relief to such areas; but famine and disaster are inevitable anyway. Such countries belong to the "can't be saved" category.

Second, there are countries that do not need assistance to survive. These are the less developed countries with ample reserves of energy and raw materials that can muster up enough foreign exchange to buy food on the world market even at increased prices; Libya, Kuwait, and other nations with extensive oil resources would be examples of countries falling in the "won't need help" group.

Finally, there are the countries that really should get help, that is, those that have successful population policies and are becoming more self-sufficient in terms of food supplies. A country may face temporary difficulties; but if its development policies reflect economic self-discipline, courage, commitment, and imagination on the part of its leaders and an acceptable degree of success in reducing fertility, it should receive assistance. South Korea and Taiwan might be cited as examples, supposing they should face food problems.

Professor P. M. Hauser has also argued that, since foreign aid is by definition limited, choices must be made now and in the future, though he does point to the dangers of such erroneous classification as would condemn a country forever, should the "triage" system be adopted despite the likelihood of its achieving self-sufficiency. He equally feels that although population factors are immensely important, other criteria should also receive weight. The managers of a development aid effort or simply of a food aid program should, in his view, adopt a more holistic approach by taking account of social, economic, and political factors like a society's ability to exploit opportunities for economic growth, the productiveness of the overall economy, and the quality of political leadership and institutions.

High Fertility Means Credit Unworthiness

Many low-income countries with exploding populations have also an exploding international debt—which brings us to the question of whether these developing countries with high demographic growth rates should qualify for grants, loans, or credits. Since 1945 the more developed nations have regularly expanded their official aid programs in terms of grants, "soft" (low-interest) loans, government export credits, and the like, while international agencies such as the International Bank for Reconstruction and Development have been set up to supply long-term loans to the "deserving." The total flows of funds (including private investment) from the developed to the less developed countries passed the $11 billion-per-year mark in the late 1960s. Desirable as these flows may be (they speed up the accumulation of productive equipment, and hence economic growth, in the less developed countries), the question arises whether these countries will ever be able to pay the necessary interest and dividends, and ultimately to repay whatever loans they received. If present trends continue, the less developed countries may in some fifteen years be so placed that the dollar cost of servicing and extinguishing their debts to the developed countries will reach the same amount as what the latter are willing to give or invest in them. Writers like the late Professor S. Enke, former consulting economist to *Tempo*, have raised the question of whether the less developed countries will then still be willing to play the game by the bankers' rules.

The capacity of a low-income country to face the burden of service and amortization depends on various factors such as the wisdom of its investments, its ability to increase output and incomes, and its capacity to augment domestic savings, tax revenues, and exports. As was earlier explained, in Chapter 8, serious complications arise on all these points through rapid population expansion, which increases a low-income country's need for capital but at the same time impedes saving, capital formation, growth of exports, and the like. In fact, the chances that a low-income country with a population growth rate of, say, 3 percent will be able to service and repay its foreign debts are pretty slim, especially if it keeps borrowing and investing. It has therefore been argued that the lending agencies and programs of the more developed countries should tie aid to the establishment and/or expansion of population control programs; the recipient countries should, after all, show their willingness to help themselves, and there is hardly a better way to do so than to embark on an energetic population control program, which will enhance the prospects for successful economic development and improve credit-worthiness. Against that argument it has been suggested that such a condition might create bad feelings in the recipient country. True as that may be, any lending country or agency is bound to evaluate a potential recipient's present and future credit-worthiness, and since future inability to service and repay debts is much aggravated by high fertility, why court almost certain embarrassment and default by lending to such a country? Some kind of "triage" might well be in order for loans, grants, and credits as well as for food aid programs.

15

Population policy: Issues and solutions

Come, my friends, 'tis not too late to seek a newer world.

Alfred Lord Tennyson

I see this both as a question of the human right of the child not to be born unless he can be properly fed, cared for and educated, have gainful employment and lead a satisfactory life, as well as the right of the population as a whole not to be burdened with unsolvable problems created by increases due to public and private health measures.

Lee Kuan Yew

Good medicine tastes bitter.

Old Japanese saying

Population Policy: What It Is and What It Does

At the end of a book like this, one naturally expects some suggestions as to what might be done to manipulate human fertility, which in many countries is high enough to impinge on the quality of human life.

Population policy is not something that can be considered in isolation. In many countries, the point at issue is one of "overall backwardness" and not merely one of population. Steps taken to affect "primitive" (high) fertility should therefore be taken in conjunction with other measures, of which land reform or many of the others previously discussed might be cited as examples.

A mere "showering" of peasant populations with pills and condoms is not likely to be successful in lowering fertility, although this is precisely the approach which the Agency for International Development seems to favor.

The economist-demographer Frank Lorimer has defined population policy or planning as a national commitment and will to deal realistically and effectively with the demographic variable in all national planning.

Sociologist P. M. Hauser has made a useful distinction among conception control, fertility or birth control, family planning, and population control. Conception control denotes all methods that prevent conception. It includes behavioral, chemical, and surgical means. Fertility or birth control includes conception control, but it embraces abortion as well. Family planning merely helps couples to have the number of children they want, which can be a large or small number; it therefore provides couples with the facilities and means enabling them to realize their desired family size. Population control, finally, comprises fertility control but also the control of in- and out-migration. It intends to exert influence on the rate of population growth. Population policy as defined above would involve population control itself.

Possible Objectives of Population Policy

Presently very few nations have a *consistent*, all-encompassing population policy. Many countries do, however, have policies that contain *some* elements of population policy. Often such programs are aimed at a maximum reduction of the death rate and at an increase in the span of life. Although for human and other reasons it seems sensible to embark on a health improvement program, if nothing is done to bring down the birthrates as well, a brutal encounter with famine may be in prospect. This seems to be the case with too many countries.

Besides maximum reduction of the death rate, a country may attempt to increase or decrease the birthrate. If the population is felt to be too small for whatever purposes the nation's leaders have in mind, fertility may be encouraged by positive measures such as family allowances, tax favors, or marriage loans or by repressive measures such as laws against birth control or discrimination against bachelors or childless couples. France, for instance, has a system of rather lavish family allowances (periodically eroded by inflation) in order to promote larger families, while in 1974 when Argentina took a fascist turn, its leaders apparently felt that the demographic growth rate of 1.4 percent was not high enough and thus closed the nation's family-planning clinics and forbade the advocacy of any means of birth control. The promoters of birth planning, it was argued, deformed the fundamental maternal function of the woman while distracting Argentina's youth from its natural duty as protagonists of the future of the fatherland. Hitler and Mussolini's repressive birth control laws were justified in almost identical language. Other nations, such as Singapore, actively attempt to depress their birthrates by measures that will be discussed later in this chapter.

A country may also try to increase or reduce the size of its population through the promotion of immigration and emigration. Australia and Canada have for many years had policies that favored immigration, while such countries as the Netherlands sponsored emigration for several years after 1945.

Sometimes policies merely aim at the discouragement of extra-marital births because it is felt that it is desirable that children grow up in normal families. Sexual education in schools is often presented as a device to discourage births out of wedlock.

Policies can also aim at reduction of the family size of the lowest-income groups, which are usually also the least educated. The argument is that the poor and ignorant get stuck with cruelly large families. Conveniently located birth control clinics staffed by people who understand the poor and are able to speak their language are often thought of as an important measure, especially if they provide contraception and abortion cheaply or freely.

In the United States some 5 million women are estimated to be in need of publicly supported family planning services.

A Note on the History of Population Policy

Contrary to what one might believe, ancient and modern history are full of examples of natalist and antinatalist policies or customs.

In the past, tribal societies have often practiced prolonged abstention from intercourse after the birth of a child. In certain areas, Javanese peasants still observe a two-year period of abstention after the birth of each child. Abortion and infanticide have been freely resorted to in the past. On certain isles in the Pacific, a woman habitually kept only between two and four of her children, taking the life of others immediately after birth. Such customs were enforced by tribal regulations that allowed them in order to maintain an equilibrium between numbers and their life-supporting environment.

In many of the known agrarian societies of Asia and the Middle East, celibacy and postponement of marriage were unknown. This enhanced the increase of numbers, but again primitive means of conception control such as abortion and infanticide were quite common.

Throughout the eighteenth and most of the nineteenth century the Japanese population remained stationary. Nongrowth was attained by such unwritten rules as those that made it shameful for a gentleman to have more than three children. The peasants on their part practiced what was called *Makibi*, meaning "thinning out." In practice this amounted to infanticide and abortion. The Meiji regime made these customs illegal.

The Roman Empire made some efforts to increase birthrates, and several laws were enacted to that effect. The Lex Julia of 18 B.C. and the subsequent Lex Papia Poppaea of A.D. 9 set up an entire system of incentives and deterrents prompting free citizens—especially the members of middle and upper classes—to reproduce. Large families received financial rewards whereas limitations were placed on the unmarried and childless.

With the advent of Christianity, abortion and infanticide became illegal although they continued to be practiced. Contraceptive techniques were crude and inefficient and their use was also discouraged by canon law. But in medieval Europe, early marriage was discouraged by certain laws and customs that shortened the reproductive period. Compulsory apprenticeship is an example. Marriage was only permitted after its termination. Many took the monastic vows and remained sterile. This, combined with the high death rates previously discussed, kept European rates of population growth low.

Between 1450 and 1750, Europe embarked on a "commercial revolution" that occurred within the framework of a politico-economic system called mercantilism. This period, notable for the emergence

and consolidation of strong nation-states, was basically natalistic in
orientation. The Black Death and the Hundred Years' War (1337-
1453) ravaged the population of Europe. Besides, writers and politicians of the period widely believed that large populations guaranteed
the wealth and security of the young, ambitious, and often threatened
nation-states. Numbers provided the basis for large armies and strong
fleets, while at the same time providing cheaply the manpower to
equip the factories.

Pronatalist policies were widely attested. Some nations, like France
and Spain, encouraged early marriages by a system of tax exemptions.
Others, such as France, gave premiums to very large families. Countries like Spain, Prussia, and Austria gave special rights and privileges
(temporary tax exemptions, pieces of land, help in finding places for
settlement, loans, and so on) to immigrants in order to encourage
their establishment. Simultaneously, a number of countries such as
Spain, France, Prussia, and Switzerland attempted to stop emigration. In France's Canadian colonies, marriage was encouraged by
bounties; large families were financially rewarded; young women
from France were shipped in to provide the settlers with brides; and
the highly profitable fur trade was forbidden to bachelors.

The eighteenth and nineteenth centuries showed growing indifference toward comprehensive population policies, although not toward
population theory, which in fact began to bloom during that period.
The twentieth century witnessed the reintroduction of comprehensive
population policies.

When in 1870-1871 France was defeated by Prussia, a number of
social scientists and popular workers were alarmed by the higher fertility levels in Prussia. A powerful and effective pronatalist pressure
group, *L'Alliance nationale pour l'accroissement de la population
francaise*, was established in 1896, and laws to suppress contraception
went into effect in 1920 and 1923. During the 1920s and 1930s family
allowances and other privileges for families with children were first
introduced, and even today France's population policy is still offi-
cially pronatalist.

The second country to introduce a pronatalist population policy
was fascist Italy. In order to conquer and man the empire that Italy
coveted, millions of extra people were needed. Repressive measures
such as the prohibition of abortion and of sales of contraceptives were
introduced after 1927. Bachelors, childless and small families had to

pay a supplementary tax, and discrimination against bachelors was practiced in all government appointments. Among the positive measures, Italy's leaders introduced marriage loans, tax favors to large families, family allowances, and special privileges for prolific mothers, while marks of public approval for very large families abounded in the state-controlled newspapers.

In the 1930s Nazi Germany and fascist Japan, which both needed manpower for their armies, factories, and their empires yet to be conquered, more or less copied the various measures Italy had introduced. Sweden, which in 1934 had a relatively low birthrate of 13.7 per thousand and a gross reproduction rate of 0.815, became preoccupied with a possible decline of population and introduced (at the recommendation of Alva and Gunnar Myrdal) a population policy that contained some positive but no repressive elements. Birth control was accepted, abortion liberalized; but marriage loans at low interest rates were introduced. Besides, maternity grants and special provisions for fatherless children and orphans were instituted. At present most countries by far still have no population policy, although the number of countries actively rejecting family planning is now small and diminishing. In a number of countries governments actively support family planning but refuse to go beyond that. As will be explained in the following section, family planning alone will not result in substantial fertility declines in nations that are in the earlier stages of their modernization process.

Why Family Planning Fails to Stop Population Growth

Very few countries presently have a comprehensive population policy aimed at a stationary population. The more developed countries have done very little in the field of population control. Since the middle of the nineteenth century, however, people became increasingly motivated by socioeconomic conditions to reduce the size of their families, although as noted previously, this has not prevented the populations of many of these countries from growing far beyond self-sufficiency levels. At present the birthrate in all more developed countries is low and still falling, and may stabilize at levels that approximately ensure a stationary population.

In the less developed countries people are often weakly motivated or not motivated at all to reduce the size of their families. Family planning does not attempt to influence the cost-benefit analysis of the couples in their reproductive years. As stated earlier, family planning helps couples to achieve the desired family size, which can actually be very large and run counter to the long-term interests of the nation. Family planning merely wants couples not to have unwanted children but generally endorses their existing reproductive objectives. For this reason there is very little hope that current family-planning programs will succeed in bringing the ongoing population growth under control. As Professor Kingsley Davis has convincingly argued, the introduction of family-planning programs (and very few governments are presently willing to go beyond it) may actually be dangerous in the sense that it may lull governments and peoples to sleep. The impression is created that adequate measures are being taken to bring down population growth, whereas in fact little is achieved to bring births into line with the requirements of the nation's present and future welfare.

Current family-planning types of policies invariably entrust the organization of programs to medical personnel, people who are trained to think in terms of health clinics, contraceptives, and the like, but who usually have only limited understanding of the far-reaching political, social, cultural, and economic changes necessary to motivate couples to reduce the size of their families. In conclusion, family planning allows families to have the number of children they desire, but does nothing to harmonize the interests of the family and the nation. In many developed and less developed countries, socio-economic reforms plus a system of sanctions and rewards is needed to bring individual and collective interests into line. All this is not to condemn the family-planning approach; for as a first step it still may be the best, and it is often politically the most suitable one. The advocates of family planning can point to the gains in maternal and child welfare its introduction will bring and thus contribute to its political acceptability.

Institutional Reforms That Depress Fertility

A first method that high-fertility countries could use to bring down their rate of increase would consist of the popularization of the small family. In the past, too many societies have exerted pressure on couples with few children, who were stigmatized as selfish, egoistic, too self-involved, and so on. The origin of such social pressures to have larger families dates from the times when death rates rivaled birth-rates and high fertility levels were needed to prevent a community's extinction. Many countries, including India, China, South Korea, and Hong Kong, already use the media to give publicity to the small family. Films, radio, and TV can also be used to present the parents of small families as the ones who loyally cooperate with the nation's needs and even the requirements of humanity as a whole. Such presentations, if continued long enough, may create a climate of opinion very favorable to population control.

Governments can also persuade the newspapers to present periodical advertisements that display the small family as the ideal one. Governments could give substantial annual rewards to short-story writers who in their stories gave the best presentation of the personal and social advantages of the small family. The incentive is thus created to write such stories, which even in semiliterate populations enjoy great popularity.

The cooperation of schoolteachers must be enlisted, and relevant textbooks should present the problems faced by a country with a fast-growing and dense population, as well as the need for and advantages of family limitation. The media and schools should also be used to provide better information on the sharply declining mortality rate. Couples should be made to realize that mortality and especially infant mortality rates have dropped substantially, so that it is no longer necessary to produce a large number of offspring in order to have at least a few survivors.

A second change that a number of countries could fruitfully bring into effect is the raising of the age of marriage, which tends to reduce the reproductive period. The reproductive period of the woman lasts about thirty years, but the years between eighteen and thirty are the most fertile. Delayed marriage can be brought about by propaganda, direct legislation, or the imposition of differential fees, that is, a very high one for the young marriages and a much lower one for couples which have the "socially approved" age.

In 1965 the Indian economist-demographer S. N. Agarwala calculated that if the average age of marriage of women were to be raised from the existing 15.6 years to 20 years, the birthrate would fall by around 29 percent within three decades. Unfortunately, in India the tendency is rather toward discussion and talk about such issues than toward action and its enforcement. Deferment of marriage has the additional advantage that women will have more time to acquire a better training or education and to develop a more prudent point of view with regard to childbearing.

A third institutional reform that helps to depress fertility is the abolition of child labor. Difficult as it may be to pass *and* enforce child labor laws in traditional peasant societies, such laws do alter the cost-benefit framework within which couples make their decisions. Especially if withdrawal of children from the labor market is combined with extended compulsory education, the costs of raising the child increase sharply, whereas the benefits decline as they no longer contribute to the family income. Just before the end of the last century, the French economist Paul Leroy-Beaulieu had already observed that the suppression of child labor and compulsory education of the young had lowered fertility in Western Europe.

In order to provide women with alternatives to childbearing, women may also be encouraged to seek gainful employment—another proven idea. In the Communist countries it is taken for granted that women join the labor force. This contributes to the relatively low fertility in most of these nations. In the non-Communist countries it is only in the highly industrialized ones that women work *en masse*. Although it may be difficult for governments to provide employment directly, they can at least strongly oppose discrimination against employment of women and they can encourage girls and young women to develop vocational interests to get involved in formal education, which both create interests other than housekeeping and childbearing. Again, economist Leroy-Beaulieu observed long ago that the emancipation of women, their gainful employment, and a more career-oriented outlook made marriage and maternity less desirable and hence reduced fertility.

A last institutional change we will contemplate here is the promotion of greater spatial and social mobility. There is a great deal of evidence that in societies where it is impossible or too difficult to improve one's status, fatalism tends to prevail and motivation toward smaller families is lacking. If, however, upward mobility is existent and made visible by successful citizens, ambitions are prompted and the willingness to make sacrifices often increases. Because a small family evidently facilitates a man's ascent, people are motivated to make greater efforts to keep their families small. As early as 1890 the

French social scientist Arsène Dumont published a book in which he claimed that in democratic regimes that combine political equality with social and economic inequality, man's desire to move upward was enhanced, especially when, as was the case in Western Europe, abundant opportunities for socioeconomic advancement existed. As a consequence of this combination of factors, people tended to prolong their education, postpone marriage, and reduce family size. A government that intends to promote such social mobility should pass laws prohibiting any kind of discrimination and should oblige its own agencies and encourage business firms to hire people only on the basis of their capacities and training. Such institutional changes as we have proposed merely set the framework within which a fertility reduction may come about. In order to accelerate the process, we need a set of incentive schemes designed specifically to upset and modify the existing decision-making process of fertile couples.

Ethical Justification of Fertility-Depressing Schemes

A common objection against fertility-reducing proposals such as tax reforms, incentive schemes, or direct restrictions on procreation is that couples should have the liberty to have all the children they want and that interference with this basic freedom is unethical. It should be clear from the preceding chapters what the flaw in this argument is; namely, that the unrestricted freedom of a couple to have all the children it wants jeopardizes the freedom and welfare of the remainder of the population. The procreating couple does not in many cases pay the full price of its procreative activities, in the same manner as the polluting individual shifts part of the costs of his activities onto others. The complete freedom of A to procreate may drive up prices, lower living standards, reduce recreation space, generate war, crime, revolutions, and pollution—all conditions which B or his children must suffer. Hence the defense of the absolute freedom of the couple to decide on its own family size has as much justification as the defense of the individual's freedom to poison the air, rivers, and lakes.

Even many tribal communities understood this, and certain tribes did, therefore, allow each mother only a restricted number of children. Yet in a democratic society it seems preferable to have population policies that at least restrict individual freedom as little as possible.

Conditions an Effective Incentive System Must Fulfill

As stated above, an incentive system should not unduly restrict individual freedom. Secondly, it should be equitable in the sense that the system should not be too oppressive for the low-income groups and it should, if possible, not penalize children. Besides, the system should be efficient, administratively feasible, and politically acceptable, while the costs of the system in a less developed country should not be exorbitant because "poverty is the biggest problem in poor countries." One has to recognize that it is not possible to satisfy all the prerequisites simultaneously, and political leaders resolved to tackle the population problem seriously have no choice but to increase the costs of childbearing, reduce the benefits of procreation, and augment the rewards for voluntary sterility. This inevitably implies that hard and unpopular choices must be made. There is no known plan that does not have some disadvantages. Tough opposition will have to be faced, and political leaders will need all their courage and conviction to push on with such measures. They should consistently remind their opponents of the alternatives to population control.

Desired Target Number

The first step a government should take is to set up the desired target number of children per family. If the authorities want zero population growth in the long run, the number of children per family required for replacement lies between two and three, depending on the mortality rate; for the United States, replacement will be achieved at 2.2 children per family or 220 children per 100 completed families. Hence the two-child family should become the norm, while some families of three (or more) children would still be needed in order to make up for those who have less than two. Governments that want to reduce a population which has grown too large should therefore set their target below replacement levels. Incentives and deterrents have the same function as sanctions in a legal system. Sanctions serve the purpose of bringing actual behavior closer to the established norm or of harmonizing societal interest with individual interests. Incentives and deterrents, therefore, should bring the actual number of children per completed family as close as possible to the desired target number.

A distinction is sometimes made between positive incentives, which are payments rewarding families that do not exceed the desired target number, and negative incentives (or disincentives), which suppress customary benefits or impose greater costs on those who surpass the desired target number. It is not possible to discuss in a short work of this kind all incentives proposed in the population literature. We will limit ourselves to some of the best-known and most imaginative proposals.

Positive Incentives

A first proposal would be an incentive payment for deferment of marriage, which would shorten the reproductive period and thus reduce fertility. Suppose the law has fixed the minimum age of marriage at eighteen years; then an annual reward could be given to each young woman or man who postponed marriage by another year. A second idea would be to give a cash payment to married couples of reproductive age for each year that they avoid procreation. A similar proposal has been made to deposit a certain sum on a blocked savings account for every woman who remains nonpregnant during a one-, two-, or five-year term. The money would be released at the end of her reproductive period. The costs of such policies may be high, but their justification lies in the fact that with each foregone birth, society has to make fewer demographic investments. A major problem is that such procedures may be too difficult to administer in those less developed countries whose administrative agencies are overburdened.

Much easier to manage would be a bonus program for permanent voluntary sterilization, with vasectomy being the obvious target; India has already tried such programs on a regional basis. The premium, which can be paid in cash or in kind, should be related to the number of children the person already has. Individuals with small families of, say, two children would get a large reward, which would become a little smaller with each additional child. The fear has been expressed that in certain less developed countries, vasectomy programs might be open to misuse and corruption.

The least the more developed countries could do, at least if they have a well-run health plan, is to reimburse the costs of sterilization to parents with poverty-level incomes who voluntarily accept it.

One reason why desired family size is often large in the less developed countries is that incomes are often too small for savings, while institutionalized old-age support is nonexistent. Accordingly parents rely on their sons for assistance in their later years. This situation would call for the establishment of social security support in old age for those persons who do not exceed the socially desired target number of children. Or, if a nation can afford it, everyone could be made eligible for support in old age; but those who have the socially desired number of children would get substantially higher benefits in compensation for the foregone sons and their potential support. Such a system would probably substantially contribute to the destruction of the incentive toward large families in traditional peasant societies. A social security system of the kind here proposed would be expensive, and its administration might be too burdensome for a less developed country. However, its costs would be justified by the birth reductions it would occasion and the investment burdens avoided. Support for the aged would have to be financed with tax receipts and would therefore compete with other important forms of government expenditure such as education or the building of transport systems. However, if the long-run view is taken, the system would more than pay for itself; its benefit-cost ratio is likely to be highly positive.

A variant of the above-mentioned social security is the Ridker plan, named after the economist Ronald Ridker. Again the aim is to express society's gratitude to all, and especially to the poor, who kept their families small, and compensate them for the foregone support in the form of working sons. The Ridker plan consists essentially in offering young couples who agree not to exceed the target number of children (or agree to a specific limit of their family size) a bond that is payable at approximately the time the couple retire or at the end of their reproductive period, whichever is sooner. The bond would become void if the couple exceeded the specified number of children. As Ridker points out, the administration of the system is simple and, therefore, well adjusted to the needs of a less developed country. Only two contacts with the administration are necessary—the first when the couple accepts the bond (which can then be fingerprinted) and the second at the time of maturity. In a slightly different manner one could imagine two types of bonds, a more sizable one for couples who accept a limit of two children and a smaller one for three-children families. An added advantage of the scheme is that it leaves couples free to determine their own contraceptive method.

Negative Incentives

A first negative incentive that is often proposed is to impose a tax on higher-order births. A justification for taxing the larger families is that they put the heaviest burdens on the community's resources. This entitles society in its turn to impose an additional burden on the more prolific parents.

An example of such a charge would be a percentage tax on the combined adjusted gross income of the parents effective until retirement. Normally, under such a system, the first two children would not be taxed; but as an example a 2 percent levy would be imposed for a third child, a 4 percent charge for a fourth, 6 percent for a fifth, and so on. In this manner, the parents of a four-child family would face a total of 6 percent tax on their adjusted gross revenue. The tax would provide the incentive for rich and poor not to exceed the target number of children if it was set at two. The tax would also speak clear language and reflect the community's values regarding the desired number of children. It would also motivate all income groups, because the rich would pay more than the poor. Besides, the tax would bring pressure on couples during the entire reproductive period. Those who had three or more children before the measure went into effect would be exempted, and adopted children would not be regarded as higher-order children so that the tax would not apply to them. The question may be asked whether the tax would really penalize the parents rather than the children. We can only be uncertain about the answer. Such a tax system would probably be more revelant in the more developed countries; in the less developed the low-income groups may be too impoverished to pay taxes anyhow and the costs of collection may be too high.

A more moderate proposal consists of the modification of the income tax laws in the sense that the number of personal exemptions allowable for children would be limited to two. In the United States this idea is also known as the Packwood plan because Senator Robert Packwood has proposed a bill eliminating deductions after the second child. In order to make the plan fair, it should not apply to adopted children or children born before acceptance of the plan. In the United States the economic impact would be rather small. Uncle Sam allows a $750 deduction per child; hence a family that earns between $8,000 and $12,000, and therefore falls in the 22 percent bracket, gets for each child a net addition of $165 to its disposable income, while a family in the $10,000 to $20,000 category finds itself in the 28 percent bracket—the net worth of the child being now $210. Compared to the total annual costs of rearing a child, these amounts are insignificant; but, as Garrett Hardin has argued, the symbolic, "educational" significance of the plan may be great.

Other writers have pleaded in favor of a total abolition of the personal exemption. In almost all Western countries, the tax system discriminates against bachelors and childless families and there is no reason to perpetuate a discriminatory system, especially in a crowded world like ours.

Another idea we will discuss in this context consists of the withdrawal of certain welfare benefits when the number of children exceeds the desired target number. At present, as in the past, most social security systems encourage fertility. The old Poor Laws of eighteenth-century England gave more assistance to large families than to small ones and thus encouraged fertility and hence the production of more poor people. Contemporary systems are often as unskillfully designed as the old Poor Laws. There have been a number of initiatives in various states to offer parents a choice of undergoing sterilization or withdrawal of welfare benefits once a given number of children was attained. Obviously those initiatives were mainly directed at low-income parents on welfare who keep having children to be brought up at the taxpayer's expense. There are families in the United States that have been on welfare for four generations. These initiatives have failed so far. From the viewpoint of political acceptability they are weak measures, as they provoke very emotional reactions such as charges of Hitlerism and disguised attempts to exterminate minority groups. The latter are usually the poorest and therefore the most likely to be on welfare.

Diminishing welfare benefits with each additional child is also a rather inept and inhumane measure, because its full weight is likely to fall on the innocent child rather than on the guilty parents. It would, we think, be far preferable to distinguish between welfare mothers who did, and those who did not, exceed a target of, say, two or three children and reward the latter category with higher old-age benefits when the day comes.

A last measure, one which in our view deserves strong recommendation, consists in the imposition of a welfare ceiling per family regardless of family size. If a ceiling on welfare grants per family is established no matter how many children there are, the welfare family is placed on an equal footing with the nonwelfare working family where additional children are usually not accompanied by extra income, with the result that the birth of another child produces a decline in the living standard of all family members. A welfare system that gives additional allowances for each extra child thus discriminates against the nonwelfare working family, which usually pays the taxes to keep the system going. The Supreme Court apparently approves of the notion of a ceiling on welfare benefits per family. In *Dandridge* v. *Williams* (397 U.S. 471 [1970]), the Supreme Court upheld the decision of a Maryland welfare regulation that imposed such a ceiling; the court argued that the state had the lawful option to appropriate limited welfare funds in this manner.

The Issue of Immigration

Population policy aiming at population control should also include due consideration of the phenomenon of immigration. In the world as a whole, the large-scale migrations of the nineteenth-century type have ceased to exist. We will limit our discussion to the case of the United States.

The immigration history of the United States is well known. Immigration before 1825 amounted to less than 10,000 persons per annum; between 1820 and 1860 some 5 million individuals landed on American shores, while between 1860 and 1920 some 28.5 million foreigners were admitted, a number that almost equals the U.S. population in 1850. Restrictive legislation came in the 1920s, and after 1929 the number of immigrants was limited to just over 150,000 per year; the McCarran-Walter Act of 1952 maintained that ceiling. Later legislation facilitated the entrance of political refugees, alien wives, and so on, and in 1957, 236,867 immigrants entered.

The Immigration Act of 1965 ended a 44-year-old tradition of using national origin as one of the major criteria for admitting people. The act established a maximum of 170,000 visas per annum for the non-Western Hemisphere nations, whereas the ceiling for the Western Hemisphere was set at 120,000. Other intricate modifications of the older laws were made. An annual average of about 290,000 persons were admitted between 1961 and 1965. The number rose to 375,000 between 1966 and 1972. In 1973 (fiscal year) it was a little higher, and for 1974 the Department of Commerce gives the figure of about 372,000. With a total monthly increase of population of about 151,000 and a monthly immigration of 31,000, the inflow of persons accounts for about 20 percent of the total population increase and approximately 25 percent of the natural monthly increase (deaths minus births), estimated at 120,000. The largest sending countries to the United States (1972 figures) are now Mexico (over 60,000 per year), the Philippines (around 25,000), Italy and China (each with just over 20,000). Korea, India, and Cuba come next with totals of 15,000 to 20,000. With the exception of Italy, most immigrants come from the less developed countries. Added to the legal immigrants are the illegal ones, who are entering in ever-growing quantities. According to conservative estimates, there are now at least 4.5 million illegal aliens living in the United States; but unofficial estimates suggest that the number could be as high as 8 million. Within ten years that number is expected to rise to at least 15 million; the annual number of illegal entrants may already have topped 1 million per year, 90 percent of these "gate-crashers" coming from Mexico; many of them pay no taxes but do enjoy welfare benefits and sometimes unemployment compensation while their children go to state-subsidized schools. The costs to the taxpayer runs into hundreds of millions of dollars. Now that the recession deepens (1975), there is a rising concern about these illegal aliens who occupy jobs (at least 1 million) that could go to un-employed American citizens who now live on welfare, unemployment benefits, or both.

The Immigration Issue Demands Reexamination

As population-related problems make themselves increasingly felt, a reorientation of immigration policies seems inevitable. Immigration adds to population growth as entrants become part of the overall population growth. At the same time, the fertility of immigrants is usually higher than that of the resident population, because most immigrants now come from less developed countries with high fertility patterns. In 1970 the average number of children born to the average American woman on completion of her reproductive period was 2.9, while it was 4.4 per resident woman of Mexican origin.

As Garrett Hardin has argued, the descendants of immigrants inevitably help to speed up the destruction of the environment in which the children and grandchildren of contemporary residents will live. The present generation cannot shun its obligation to protect this environment to the best of its knowledge for future generations. In the short run, immigrants add to the existing welfare burden because many of them are poorly skilled and unemployment among them is high. Besides, immigrants create social conflicts, as they live in unfamiliar social and linguistic surroundings. Race conflicts are also generated now that most immigrants come from Latin America, the Caribbean countries, and Asia.

It has been said that receiving immigrants from the less developed countries helps to relieve their population pressures. If we take that argument seriously, the United States and other immigrant-receiving nations should accommodate at least 53 million people per year, which is the annual excess of births over deaths in all less developed nations. Besides, welcoming immigrants from other nations may not be the correct method of helping them, because some of these nations may postpone painful yet inevitable adjustments as long as they have the impression that they can export their population problem to other countries. At present, few of the less developed countries sincerely attempt to bring their population growth really under control.

Industrial northwestern Europe has also become a receiving area of migrants. In 1971 about 8 million migrants worked in those countries. It was often argued that these industrialized countries faced "labor shortages" that slowed down economic growth. It was said that with the help of foreign workers these nations could accelerate that growth. Immigration, therefore, was highly beneficial. The argument is, it seems, founded on questionable wisdom. Is it wise to solve a short-run labor-shortage problem by creating a long-term population problem? And what if these countries had not relied on foreign labor to combat the labor shortage? In that case a number of unproductive marginal firms would have been eliminated, as they would have been unable to hire workers at going wage rates. Wages would have risen faster, a fact that the domestic laborers would certainly have appreciated. The increased salaries and wages would have provided employers with the incentive to economize on labor by adopting labor-saving equipment, which in turn would have stimulated research in and production of such apparatus. The rate of technological progress and innovation would in all probability have been higher. Moreover, what does a labor shortage show but the unwillingness or the inability (or both) of governments to moderate aggregate demand? During the 1960s production in northwestern Europe was usually near or at its peak. Governments, however, kept increasing their levels of spending substantially, which had inflationary effects as the level of spending began to exceed the available production of goods and services at existing prices. Instead of practicing financial restraint, governments created huge budget deficits that were financed with newly created money. The aggregate excess demand for commodities and services created a labor shortage. Instead of importing foreign workers, governments should have used fiscal and monetary policies to dampen the inflationary pressures; but political leaders apparently lacked the courage and will to tackle that problem seriously.

Professor E. J. Mishan has convincingly argued that migrant labor does not reduce inflationary pressures by adding to output or aggregate supply. Migrants' labor does increase the production in the receiving countries, but even foreign workers have needs. If they spend all their income in the receiving country, they augment aggregate demand by what they contribute to total supply. If they save something out of their income, the addition to demand will be less; but since their incomes are usually low, there is not much opportunity for saving. If they send some of their savings abroad in the form of remittances, a balance-of-payments problem may be created, although in the 1960s there was little evidence of such a problem. However, an influx of foreign labor may stimulate private business investment and is certain to cause higher public outlays on overhead. New schools and houses must be built, more transport facilities are needed, and so on. All this adds to the total demand for investment and consumer goods; hence it cannot be argued that foreign labor helps to combat inflationary pressures.

It is interesting to observe that in the United States few people dare to question existing immigration policies. As Hardin puts it, those who point to the negative aspects of continued immigration are readily accused of selfishness, isolationism, racial prejudice, bigotry, and other evils. In Europe, governments have mostly been unresponsive to indications that in their respective countries citizens reacted negatively to foreign immigration. In spite of innumerable private and public manifestations not to allow more immigrants in such countries as Switzerland, France, the Netherlands, the United Kingdom, and Germany, the governments kept inviting foreign workers during the 1960s.

Singapore: Population Policy in Action

The Republic of Singapore is the only nation outside the Communist world that has shown the will and the capacity to reduce fertility fast and drastically and can now point to the lowest population growth rate in Asia (after Japan), that is, 1.6 percent. The island city-state is multiracial, with the Chinese population dominating (76.2 percent). Prime Minister Lee Kuan Yew's People's Action Party has been in the saddle since 1959. The nation's institutions are democratic and its economy is based on market mechanisms and free enterprise. Its per capita income is the second highest in Asia (after Japan).

Family planning started on a private, voluntary basis in 1949. In 1959, when the People's party came into power, the government gave it its official support. Because of a combination of a very high "natural" birthrate of over 45 per thousand and a very low "artificial" death rate of below 8 per thousand, the annual demographic growth rate amounted to 4 percent. In 1953 immigration from China, India, and Malaysia was brought under tight control. In 1969 the inflow of people was practically reduced to zero. In the meantime the Singapore Family Planning Association continued its activities and used the media to prepare the Singapore population for the needs of family planning. In 1965 the government fully recognized the need to curtail fertility for human as well as socioeconomic reasons and its Ministry of Health assumed complete responsibility for family planning. A network of family-planning clinics was set up and two informational and educational campaigns were launched. Radio, TV, and other media were used to advocate the advantages of the small family and to increase family planning awareness. Special efforts were made to get to the lower-income groups. These endeavors were apparently crowned with success, because between 1966 and 1970 the birthrate fell from 28.6 to 21.1 per thousand, whereas the general fertility rate dropped from 157.5 to 100.7 per thousand. The number of contraceptive users rose sharply.

Abortion was liberalized in 1969 by the Abortion Act. Termination of pregnancy was authorized on medical as well as socioeconomic grounds. Applications had to be filed to an eleven-member board. Acts passed in 1969 and 1972 relaxed the requirements for male and female sterilization.

Singapore laws regarding the minimum age of marriage, child labor, and old-age security possibly help to win popular support for the small-family concept. The minimum age for marriage is eighteen, but candidates under twenty-one must have written permission from their parents or their substitutes. Child labor is no longer permitted. Until the age of twelve, a child is not allowed to be actively employed and thereafter he can only be hired to do light work. This of course reduces the economic value of children, who until age twelve cannot contribute to the family income. In both the private and public sector, old-age support is incorporated in the social security system. In the public sector the government pays the entire social security fee, whereas in the private sector both employees and employers contribute. When salaries are below a certain threshold, the employers are assessed for the whole due. This measure reduces the dependence on sons for old-age relief.

Certain specific incentive arrangements were made in 1969. Accouchement fees in the government hospitals where most children are born were set at ten Singapore dollars for the first two children. For the third child the bill was set at $ S 50 and $ S 100 for the fourth. Taxpayers could claim a $ S 750 deduction for the first child, $ S 500 for the second and third, and $ S 300 for the fourth and fifth child. The discrimination against the smaller family for admission to low-cost public housing was ended. Large families no longer enjoyed priority. This was an important measure, because some 40 percent of the Singapore population lives in such housing facilities.

THE THIRD CHILD IS A LUXURY

"For the Singapore of the 1970s, the third child is a luxury, and the fourth and fifth are antisocial acts." With these words Prime Minister Lee Kuan Yew announced the new measures taken in 1972, which were to become effective on August 1, 1973.

Income tax deductions were no longer granted for the fourth and fifth child, so that such deductions were only permitted for the first three. In the public as well as the private sector, maternity leave with pay was to be dispensed only for the first two children. Maternity costs in hospital were raised with each successive child, particularly after the third child. Those fees, however, could be waived if either of the parents accepts sterilization after the birth of their last child. Families with only two children were to be granted priority in terms of public housing. The larger families would have to wait longer in order to get a housing unit. Finally, sexual education was to be introduced as a compulsory subject in primary and secondary schools. As Lee Kuan Yew said in an interview with *People*—a periodical published by the International Planned Parenthood Federation—the remaining problem is to reach the very fertile "hard core" of those 12 to 15 percent of the Singapore population who are little educated and whose actions are still dominated by traditional beliefs. Once they can be induced to adopt low-fertility values, the population problem will be solved.

16

Contraception, past, present, and future

> *The principal point is not to have a superfluity of men, but to render those we have as little unfortunate as possible.*
>
> Voltaire

Need for New Contraceptives

History seems to indicate that fertility reduction only comes about subject to several conditions. Small families should yield tangible advantages; couples must find it normal to balance the advantages against the inconveniences of having another child; they must perceive the advantage of a small over a large family and they must have available contraceptive information and safe, simple, and inexpensive contraceptive devices, such devices having no side effects nor interfering with joyous love-making.

In such societies that have become urbanized and modernized, couples can usually perceive the advantages of fertility reduction; this is much less true in tradition-bound, predominantly agricultural societies. Hence the importance of contraceptives that require only low motivation for use.

This chapter will summarize some measures people have taken in the past to prevent coitus from resulting in pregnancy, the current state of contraception, and any new birth control agents that may be expected to emerge in the future.

Contraception Yesterday

Until recently there existed very little literature on contraception, mainly because until the time of World War I, school, church, courts, newspapers, books, and people themselves avoided any mention of sex and contraception; even medical science considered it beneath its dignity to discuss such "improper" matters. This might give the impression that contraception hardly existed, though it is perhaps actually as old as man himself. For most of his history, however, man ignored the basics of the reproductive process, his contraceptive techniques being either ineffective or only partly effective.

Two discoveries stand out from the rest. A Dutch biologist and microscopist by the name of Antony van Leeuwenhoek (1632-1723) discovered human spermatozoa. He had earlier discovered methods of grinding single lenses to give greater magnification than any others available and to enable him to see "little animals" swimming in the seminal fluid of man. But man had to await the studies of the English physician Martin Barry (1802-1855), who in the 1840s discovered that the male spermatozoa must penetrate the female egg in order to create new life.

In short, until the nineteenth century, contraceptives reflected man's imperfect understanding of the reproductive process. Below is a short list of the techniques man has tried in order to prevent pregnancy.

COITUS INTERRUPTUS

Coitus interruptus consists of withdrawal of the stimulated penis just before ejaculation. The technique is old, probably the oldest known to man. The Old Testament refers to it, which shows that the ancient Hebrews were familiar with the method. Anthropologists have noted the practice in tribal civilizations, and it has been practiced throughout the world until now.

POSTCOITAL DOUCHING

This method is at least 2,000 years old. The early Egyptians and Indians used it. Various prescriptions for the chemical content of the douche were recommended, such as a solution of water and zinc sulphate. Charles Knowlton (1800-1850), an early American writer on birth control, discussed this method in detail in his *The Fruits of Philosophy* (1832). By 1850 douching had become one of the more popular methods in England, and even in the 1930s it was still a widely practiced method in the Western countries. Its decline started after that period.

SPERMICIDES

Spermicides or pessaries are substances which are introduced into the vagina before intercourse to immobilize or neutralize the sperm on contact. They, too, have been in use for a long time, though it has sometimes been thought that they had to be introduced after, instead of before, intercourse.

Even as early as 1850 B.C. pessaries were in use in ancient Egypt. They were made of a mixture of crocodile dung and a pastelike substance such as honey. Elephant dung has been used in India for the same purpose, while over the rest of the world almost all imaginable and unimaginable raw materials have been tried by women eager to make love without making babies. Pessaries have been made from local plants in many areas, not excluding cabbage, crushed herbs, animal earwax, unripe gallnut, pomegranate, and pulp of figs.

In 1880 Walter John Rendall, a London pharmacist, produced the first pessary that was reasonably safe and had no negative side effects. His pessaries were made from quinine and cocoa butter, and soon enjoyed a widespread reputation. Today foams, foaming tablets, jellies, and creams are available on the market that contain chemicals to deactivate sperm.

CAPS, DIAPHRAGMS, AND OTHER BARRIERS

Humans have used various means to prevent sperm from entering the womb by blocking the cervix. The ancient Hebrews used the sponge, a method that apparently became popular in France in the eighteenth century and was still widely used in the 1930s. It is cheap, and the sponge can be removed by a thread attached to it.

Francis Place, a nineteenth-century English tailor who—once he had become financially independent—devoted himself to social problems, advocated this method in his pamphlets aimed at the prolific poor in the United Kingdom. It is not known whether he used the method himself; but he *did* father fifteen children (five of whom died in infancy). German-Hungarian peasants apparently used caps made from melted beeswax in the nineteenth century. A German physician by the name of Dr. Wilde applied a rubber cap for the first time, and in the early 1880s another German physician, Wilhelm Mensinga, improved and popularized this method.

CONDOMS

The sheath also has a long history. The ancient Egyptians wore colored sheaths as early as 1350 B.C., though mainly for decorative purposes. Later in history they were used as a prophylactic to protect the wearer from syphilis. The condoms were made from animal membrane (intestine, bladder, etc.). In the sixteenth century a linen version appeared in Europe; thereafter they were used as contraceptives. Dr. Condom, physician at the court of Charles II (1630-1685), discovered that the intestines of lambs suitably processed provided an appropriate material for sheaths. They could be bordered at the open end with a ribbon. Charles II, worried as he was about his ever-growing number of legitimate and illegitimate children, had asked the doctor for advice in the matter, or so goes the story.

Although they have been industrially manufactured since the eighteenth century, mass production and popularity had to await the advent of vulcanized rubber.

ORAL CONTRACEPTIVES

Oral contraceptives, like some other methods, are at least as old as recorded history, and everything under the sun has been tried or rather swallowed to prevent pregnancy. Literally hundreds of leaves, roots, seeds, and the like have been used for the purpose. Tea made from crushed willow leaves has been a popular and ineffective contraceptive in Western Europe.

Since mules are sterile, the consumption of their various parts has been supposed to produce sterility. A man's urine, dead bees, scrapings of the male deer horn, the village blacksmith's iron-containing water, spider's eggs, and snake skins have all been given a try, probably with questionable success.

Margaret Sanger, who as a nurse among the poor familiarized herself with all the miseries of unwanted pregnancy (her life story is a novel by itself), managed to convince Dr. Gregory Pincus in 1950 that he should devote his time and talents to finding a better contraceptive than those available. It occurred to Dr. Pincus that, since progesterone arrests the release of further ova, the same hormone artificially introduced might also prevent ovulation in nonpregnant women. With financial support from the Planned Parenthood Federation, and later from a pharmaceutical company, Pincus, assisted by John Rock and Celso Garcia, developed the famous "pill." Nowadays (1974) two kinds of pills are widely used: (1) the combination pill contains synthetic estrogen and progesterone; (2) the sequential pill contains only estrogen to be taken during the first part of the cycle, followed by pills containing both estrogen and progesterone. The method is reliable and a pill a day does in fact keep the babies away, because the woman's body is made to believe that it is already pregnant and ovulation ceases to occur.

RHYTHM METHOD

The "rhythm method" consists of practicing temporary abstinence from sexual relations during the fertile period. This method we owe to the discoveries of D. Ogino (Japan) and B. Krauss (Austria), who discovered independently in 1930 that ovulation occurs approximately twelve to sixteen days before the onset of the next menstrual flow. When the menstrual cycle lasts twenty-eight days, the first day of the fertile period would be day 10 and the last would be day 17. This is because sperm survival is estimated at two days and ovum survival at one day, which adds three days (two before and one after); the first time during which conception can occur establishes the total fertile period at 8 days. Many women, however, experience variations in the length of the menstrual cycle from month to month, which makes the method laborious and unreliable, and the failure rate astronomically high—15 to 30 pregnancies in 100 women using this method for one year (United States, Canada).

INTRAUTERINE DEVICES

Intrauterine devices have also been around for a long time. A kind of IUD is described in the works of Hippocrates, the ancient Greek doctor, while Arabian camel drivers for centuries knew the trick of inserting small round pebbles into the uterus of their camels to prevent them from becoming pregnant during the long journey through the desert.

In 1928 Dr. Ernst Grafenberg, a German, experimented with an intrauterine ring made of silkworm gut and later of silver wire; but it was not until the 1960s that the IUD came into renewed prominence. IUDs are now produced in a great variety of shapes and are made mostly of flexible plastics noninjurious to body tissues. It is easy to introduce the IUD into the uterus, and it prevents conception immediately thereafter.

STERILIZATION

Sterilization also has a long background. Female sterilization involves either removal of the reproductive organs or simply tubal ligation, which means tying the fallopian tubes so that the eggs cannot reach the uterus; male sterilization involves the removal of a small portion of the *vas deferens* (the canal along which the sperm travels from the testicles to the penis). The ancient Egyptians were familiar with the method of removing the ovaries in women. Australian tribes are reported to have operated on men and women's reproductive organs in order to induce sterility. Male and female sterilizations through vasectomy and tubal ligation are nowadays safe methods and have no known side effects.

What Is Available Today?

Although a large variety of contraceptive methods is now available, there is no certainty that they will be used to bring about a large-scale reduction in fertility, especially in agrarian societies where growth rates are high but motivation toward avoiding pregnancy is low.

Oral contraceptives must be taken for twenty to twenty-one days of the cycle. There are side effects, and those taking them have to be able to count and to remember to take a pill each day. Some minor side effects are nausea and weight gain, and among the more serious are blood-clotting diseases, which, though rare, do occur.

About 10 percent of all women receiving IUDs will expel them during the first year of use; in addition, bleeding, spotting, and a variety of pains are regularly reported. Between 2 and 3 percent of all IUD users will suffer from some infection of the pelvic organs. In most cases such infections can be successfully treated with antibiotics; but sometimes the device has to be removed. In many less developed countries there are simply not enough doctors around to treat complications.

Sterilization has many advantages and is a "once and for all" thing with no side effects; the fact that it is irreversible makes many people hesitate. In some countries males find the idea that they are no longer able to impregnate difficult to accept. Moreover, there are many popular misconceptions about sterilization; people sometimes confuse it with castration, or believe that it somehow reduces physical strength, sexual capacity, or desire.

As stated above, withdrawal is an ancient method, cheap and needing no devices; but it takes plenty of self-discipline on the part of the male and often leaves the woman unsatisfied.

The "rhythm method" is also cheap; and it has the blessing of the Catholic church. However, the abstinence period is at least eight days long; and it is often difficult to calculate the fertile period since most women are not always regular in the menstrual cycle. Besides, it takes a lot of motivation and determination to work out the exact time of ovulation, which may change from month to month because of individual variations in the length of the menstrual cycle.

Condoms are widely used; but they reduce sensitivity and require strong motivation, if only because the sexual foreplay has to be interrupted for the condom to be put on, while it has to be removed immediately after ejaculation.

Rubber diaphragms are quite effective, have no side effects, and have other advantages such as cheapness. However, there must be a doctor or family-planning specialist to examine the woman and to choose with her the right size of diaphragm, as they are liable to slip out of position during intercourse. To have a bathroom available is almost a *must*, and the woman must insert the device each time sex is likely.

Spermicides have a high failure rate and, although much more acceptable than those the ancient Egyptians used, can be messy, as they sometimes leak from the vagina during or after intercourse and also exude chemical smells.

Douching is an out-of-date method. It is characterized by a high failure rate, since sperm passes into the reproductive organs before douching can occur. It requires strong motivation, as douching has to take place immediately after ejaculation—which means that the woman has to leave the bed just when a process of drowsiness and relaxation is setting in. The process also demands availability of a bathroom with running hot and cold water.

Means of Fertility Control in the Future

The foregoing remarks lead us to the conclusion that we still possess no contraceptive especially fitted to the needs of the less-developed countries, where motivation to prevent conception is low. There is no "ideal contraceptive," that is, one that would be completely effective, reversible, free of all side effects, cheap, and not inimical to the spontaneity and intimacy of the love relation; nor, as our argument on new directions in this area will show, does there seem to be one on the horizon.

NEW ORAL CONTRACEPTIVES IN THE OFFING

Most new oral contraceptives are variations on the existing steroid contraceptives. One effort made is to manufacture a "pill" containing estrogens and progestins in much lower doses to reduce the known side effects of the ordinary pill. The resulting protection against pregnancy is, however, somewhat lower and the incidence of menstrual irregularities higher. Another method leaves out estrogen (which causes the side effects) altogether; these pills contain only progesterone and have been found to protect most women from pregnancy anyway. Their action on the organism is different. The "mini-pill," as this version is called, has a higher failure rate than the estrogen-containing pill, and it has also been found to cause menstrual irregularities.

The once-a-month pill provides the user with a monthly supply of estrogen and progesterone, and has the advantage that only twelve need to be taken in a year. However, the incidence of menstrual irregularity is higher than for the daily pill.

PROGESTERONE NOT TAKEN ORALLY

Tests with injections of a long-lasting progesterone have been carried out in several countries. While they may only provide full protection for three months, they usually prevent conception for a period ranging from twelve to twenty-one months. If only the existing side effects (irregular menses and the possibility of permanent sterility) were eliminated, it could be an effective method for worldwide use if countries have enough nurses and doctors to give the shots.

The progesterone implant consists of a small drug-releasing progesterone-filled capsule that slowly releases its contents and provides year-long protection. Like the progesterone injection, it is associated with irregular menstruation.

The vaginal ring, finally, consists of a silastic, progesterone-filled ring that is inserted in the vagina in the same position as the diaphragm just after menstruation and is left for twenty-one days. Upon its removal, menstruation begins, whereafter it can be reinserted. The progesterone discharged by the ring enters the bloodstream through the vaginal wall. Like all progesterone preparations, the vaginal ring provokes changes in the lining of the uterus to create a nonreceptive environment, changing the mucus secretions of the cervix to make it difficult, if not impossible, for the sperm to pass into the uterus. Progesterones are also believed to have some effect on the fallopian tubes, perhaps slowing down the movement of the ova. It seems a promising method; but, again, the woman has to be able to count, and she must also be familiar with her own reproductive organs.

NEW IUDS

Several new intrauterine devices are also being tested. Most recent types of IUDs are manufactured from inert plastic. Tests on new materials are under way. An alloy of copper and other materials is one new variation under study. The continuous erosion of the copper would create a nonreceptive environment in the uterus, preventing implementation of a fertilized ovum. The advantage over currently used IUDs is the spermicidal effect of the copper.

Experiments are also being conducted with an IUD that releases small doses of estriol, a substance that has been shown to have a high antifertility activity and one that is likely to improve the protection that existing IUDs provide.

Another type of intrauterine device now under study is made from reinforced silastic rubber. It takes the form of a pouch; after insertion into the uterine cavity, which is apparently very easy, it is filled with fluid and assumes the configuration of the uterus. This device really seems to be better tolerated than the IUDs now used, and the expulsion rate is low.

REVERSIBLE VASECTOMY

A great deal of research is being done on a method of male sterilization that would have the additional advantage of being reversible. The idea is to plug the spermatic duct instead of cutting it. The new method, like the old, would prevent sperm from being ejaculated and so cause infertility. At the moment animal experiments with valves, clips, silicone plugs, and silk thread are under way; experiments with valves in guinea pigs and dogs have shown the possibility of reversibility. If, for instance, a device is implanted in the "off" position, aspermia (zero sperm) occurs after a few weeks, and when the position of the valves is reversed, sperm transport is resumed after a short interval. Extensive further testing of these devices is necessary. Dr. Sherman J. Silber, a University of California urologist, has developed a microscopic surgical technique which so far has proved completely effective in reversing a vasectomy. He warns, however, that the technique is still an experimental stage and that for the moment vasectomy must still be regarded as a permanent procedure.

CONTRACEPTIVE ADDITIVES TO FOOD OR WATER
Much has been said and written about an oral contraceptive that could be added to food and water, just as vitamins are added to bread and milk. Such a method would be cheap. It would be efficacious in the sense that it could result in a massive fertility reduction in the less developed countries, which are facing a population explosion. Some people seem to have blind faith in such a chimerical contraceptive— despite the obvious human rights issues involved.

Such contraceptive additives raise problems that at present seem insurmountable. Were the method to be developed in the United States, for example, it would probably take a very long time and very substantial funds. Research institutes, medical schools, and the like have the capacity to make discoveries; but only the pharmaceutical companies have the specialists, funds, and facilities to develop a discovery into a fully tested drug ready for consumption. The requirements of the Federal Drug Administration for the release of a new drug are stiff, and the development costs of new chemical contraceptives have escalated during the last two decades. These rising costs are likely to retard the discovery of a contraceptive additive, as well as of other new chemical contraceptives. It would seem almost impossible to add contraceptives to water; they would presumably have to be put into the municipal water supplies, but in that case selective or voluntary use would be impossible. Moreover, such contraceptives would not reach that half of the world's population that depends on well-water.

The contraceptive additive should affect only those who are in their reproductive period, and not the young or old. An additive that stimulates hair growth on girls' chests is obviously not acceptable. Another danger is that water so treated will be consumed by farm animals and make them sterile too. Moreover, such a contraceptive must display chemical stability in contact with metals and immunity to the effects of cooking, refrigeration, and so on.

Another possibility is that of adding the contraceptive agent to certain foods. Added to a staple, it would be comparable to water, in which case we must have another drug to neutralize the sterilizing effects of the contraceptive agent for those who desire pregnancy.

But if it were added to certain foods only, then only those wanting to be sterile could consume those foods. If it were added to salt, those wishing temporary sterility would use the salt with the contraceptive additive and those wishing another birth would use untreated salt. The foods would have to be factory-produced, and only a few biochemical technicians would be required to supervise the process of adding the contraceptive agent. Such foods or "leftovers" would obviously not be given to farm animals. The method might be more acceptable and successful as a voluntary rather than a compulsory one. Yet the fact remains that there are many difficulties associated with the development of such a chemical contraceptive, and the experts in this area believe that it will take decades to come up with an agent ready for use. For a long time to come, therefore, we will have to continue to rely on contraceptive methods that, because of their defects, will require rather strong motivation for their application. Their widespread use among the little-motivated agrarian populations that inhabit most of the Asian, African, and Latin American continents is unlikely for the time being. There seems really little reason to suppose that the population explosion will be curbed by a contraceptive breakthrough.

Conclusion

The Future is Now.
Margaret Mead

I never think of the future, it comes soon enough.
Albert Einstein

Predictions about the future now abound. Few are optimistic. It is, however, important to keep in mind that the record of past forecasts is definitely poor and there is little reason to believe that present predictions are any better.

We can prognosticate, however, that world population will continue to grow rapidly and massively in the near future, thus making mankind hungrier, dirtier, more crowded, and more quarrelsome. Our environment will also continue to be wrecked, mined, and bulldozed. How long it will last is not possible to say.

In a pessimistic mood, one could argue that the path most countries now follow will lead to tragedies and catastrophes. There are too many governments that do not respond realistically to problems created by the continuous expansion of population and production. There are still nations whose governments take the view that rapid population growth is a positive force for socioeconomic development. Peru, Algeria, Albania, Cuba, Argentina, and French-speaking sub-Saharan Africa are examples. In too many countries, developed and less developed, the quality of the politicians and administrators who are running things sadly leaves much to be desired. History shows an unfortunate number of examples of political leaders who have failed to exercise even ordinary foresight. Every history book is full of testimonies to governments that refused to see the writing on the wall. And why should the future be different from the past in this respect? Not only does the average political leader inspire us with little hope; the fact that our brains seem to be made for short-term rather than for long-term thinking also seems to lead to the conclusion that we will always be unable to build a stable and sane society. People refuse to see what they do not wish to see—and the fact is that most people fail to perceive long-term threats to their existence. Unpleasant facts are evaded until that is no longer possible, and then it is often too late to prevent disaster. The scientific explanation for this well-known phenomenon is provided by the concept of "denial"—an unconscious psychological defense mechanism that is aimed at the warding off of painful or anxiety-creating perceptions. The existence of distressing facts is denied and thus kept from the consciousness.

One could argue, more optimistically, that a certain number of publications and the efforts of a number of concerned scientists have contributed to a gradual awakening of world opinion. A recent example of such publications is, of course, *The Limits to Growth*. More and more people now realize that the carrying capacity of the earth is limited and vulnerable and hence that insurmountable limits are set to the continued expansion and amplification of population and production. At the United Nations World Population Conference in Bucharest, Rumania, in August 1974 it became clear that more and more nations are becoming deeply concerned about the implications of rapid population growth, although some skeptical observers noted that during the twelve days of that conference the hungry of the world increased by about 3 million. Another hopeful fact is that a growing number of less developed countries seem to have declining birthrates. In a number of countries such as Taiwan, Hong Kong, Singapore, and South Korea, this decline seems to be accelerating. This decline in fertility seems to be closely associated with "socioeconomic development" as usually defined. Since an ever-growing number of nations is embarking on the modernization process, there is at least some reason for hope here. The periods of time the Western nations have needed to move from high birth and death rates to low ones have not been short—a matter of decades rather than years. The Central and Eastern European countries, however, started the transition from high to low vital rates much later, and had higher birthrates to begin with. The reductions of their birthrates, however, were much faster, which lends at least some support to the hypothesis that the later you start, the faster you go. We may, therefore, have at least a modest hope that there will be a number of "latecomers" who will achieve low birthrates in a relatively short period of time, especially if they complement their economic and social development with well-conceived population policies. It remains a fact, however, that there are also some big countries such as India, Pakistan, and Mexico where one might have expected a significant fertility decline and where things just do not seem to be moving that way.

This leads us to conclude that the main challenge today is to prevent the population problem from becoming truly crippling. Although it would have been desirable to tackle population-related issues many decades ago, it is not yet too late for voluntary action. The longer we wait, the more change will be forced on us by external events; we shall then have to adjust the hard way, that is, by catastrophe rather than by calculation.

Glossary

Age Composition: This term or the term "age structure" refers to the proportion of various age groups in a given population.

Aggregate Demand: The total demand for goods and services in the economy.

A.I.D.: Agency for International Development; semiautonomous unit of the State Department.

Balance of Payments: Ratio of the monetary value of all credit and debit transactions of one country to those of the rest of the world (foreign nations and international institutions).

Balance of Trade: That part of a country's balance of payments dealing with merchandise imports and exports and the buying and selling of such services as tourism, transport, and insurance.

Birthrate: Also called "crude birthrate." It consists of the number of live births per thousand people in a year.

Capital: The stock of productive equipment used in production.

Capital Deepening: The increase of capital relative to labor.

Capital Widening: The equipment of additions to the labor force with the same amount of capital the other members have.

Childbearing Age: See reproductive period.

Death Rate: Also called "crude death rate." It is the number of deaths per year per thousand people.

Demographic Investments: Expenditures aimed at preventing population growth from causing a drop in the standard of living.

Demographic Transition: The transition from a situation of high birth and death rates to one in which both these rates are low.

Demography: The scientific study of human populations primarily with respect to their size, composition, and distribution.

Density of Population: Depicts the average number of people per unit area.

Dependents: Nonproductive consumers; it includes customarily both the children under fifteen and the aged of sixty and above.

Disguised Unemployment: A situation in which part of the labor force is being used in the most efficient manner. Perhaps they only work a few hours a day; perhaps they work with outdated tools; and so on.

Economic Growth: The increase of a nation's real output of goods and services of real GNP. Sometimes a distinction is made between extensive and intensive economic growth. "Extensive" growth refers to a mere increase in total production, "intensive" growth to an increase in output per capita.

Economies of Scale: These exist when a firm's long-run costs per unit of output decline as the scale of productive capacity of the firm or industry increases. The advantages of specialization and mass production can be realized. Lower prices can be obtained by buying large quantities of raw materials and intermediate products. Larger firms can also process their by-products. More expensive, better trained executives can be hired, and so on.

Exponential Growth: The increase of a quantity by a constant percentage of the whole over a constant time period. If a population increases annually by 2 percent, we are faced with a situation of exponential growth. It means that the increase in absolute numbers is constantly greater.

Fecundity: The biological capacity to reproduce.

Fertility: The actual reproductive performance of an individual or group. The general "fertility rate" refers to the number of live births per year per thousand women of reproductive age.

Great Depression: The unprecedented decline in the level of business activity and employment during the early 1930s.

Gross National Product (GNP): The dollar value of a nation's total annual output of final goods and services.

Gross Reproduction Rate: The average number of daughters a woman will bear in the childbearing years assuming zero mortality during the reproductive years and unchanged age-specific fertility. This fertility refers to the annual number of live births per thousand women in each of seven age groups (15-19, 20-24, . . . , 45-49).

Import Duties: Taxes imposed on commodity imports.

Import Quotas: Restrictions on the number of units of a good that may be imported during a given time period (a year usually).

Income Elasticity of Demand for Food Products: This concept refers to the percentage relationship of the quantity of food demanded and the percentage change of income. It is a measure of the responsiveness of quantities bought to changes in income.

Infant Mortality Rate: Measures mortality in the first year of life. It refers to the annual deaths of children under one year of age per thousand live births during the same year.

Investment: That portion of a nation's output that goes to real capital goods or alternatively all expenditures on productive equipment such as plant and machines.

Law of Diminishing Returns: If in a production process the input level of one resource is increased by constant amounts while the other resources or factors of production are held fixed, beyond some point the resulting increments in output become smaller and smaller.

Less Developed Country: This term is used to denote a nation with a per capita income of less than $600.

Life Expectancy at Birth: The average number of years of life expected at birth under a given set of mortality conditions. Those who die early and those who die late in life are included in the average.

Machismo: Strong, assertive masculine behavior characterized by virility, self-assurance, courage. It is a quality prized above all others in Latin America.

Marginal Firm: A firm that is relatively inefficient. Its costs per unit of output are relatively high.

Mercantilism: A general body of economic doctrine that promoted nationalism, justified a policy of economic and military expansion, and emphasized the accumulation of gold and silver. It prevailed among European statesmen from the sixteenth to the latter part of the eighteenth century.

Migration: The movement from one geographic area to another; such movement involves a permanent change of residence.

More Developed Country: This term refers to nations with a per capita income of $1200 or above.

Mortality: Unless otherwise specified the term "mortality" is used as a synonym for the crude death rate.

Population Implosion: Growing concentration of people in relatively small areas.

Preventive Check: This check denotes all influences that lead to a diminution of the birthrate; birth control and celibacy are examples.

Price Cartel: Price arrangement among sellers. In essence it is a system of collusion aiming at the elimination of price competition.

Rate of Natural Increase: The annual net increase or decrease of population resulting from the difference between birth and death rates.

Repressive Check: All factors operating to increase the death rate such as, in particular, famines and epidemics.

Reproductive Period: The period during which reproduction or procreation is possible. For women this period is assumed to last from puberty to the menopause. For statistical purposes the childbearing age corresponds to the fifteen to forty-nine age span.

Savings Rate: The proportion saved out of current income.

Schizophrenia: Comprises a group of reactions characterized by odd and bizarre behavior, unexpected responses, and defects in the thinking and associative processes.

Stationary Population: A population with constant vital rates and a constant sex and age composition. The rate of increase is zero.

Unemployment: Workers without job connections.

Urbanization: The rise of the proportion of the total population concentrated in urban areas of 20,000 or more.

Vital Rates: The expression "vital rates" is restricted here to mean birth and death rates.

Selected Bibliography

Adelman, M. A. "Global Aspects of the Petroleum Situation: A Modest Proposal."
  Business Economics, Vol. IX (January 1974).

Appleman, P. *The Silent Explosion*. Boston: Beacon Press, 1965.

Baumol, W. J., and Oaks, W. E. "The Use of Standards and Press for Protection of the
  Environment." *The Swedish Journal of Economics*, Vol. LXXIII (March 1971).

Berelson, B. "Beyond Family Planning." *Studies in Family Planning*, February 1969.

Boulding, K. E. "The Economics of the Coming Spaceship Earth." In *Economic
  Growth vs. the Environment*. Edited by W. A. Johnson and J. Hardesty. Belmont,
  Calif.: Wadsworth, 1971.

Boulding, K. E. "Environment and Economics." In *Environment, Resources, Pollution and Society*. Edited by W. W. Murdoch. Stanford: Sinauer Associates, 1971.

Boulding, K. E. "The Social System and the Energy Crisis." *Science*, Vol. LXXXIV
  (April 1974).

Bouthoul, G. *La Surpopulation dans le Monde*. Paris: Payot, 1958.

Brown, L. R. *In the Human Interest*. New York: W. W. Norton, 1974.

Brown, L. R. "World Population and Food Supplies: Looking Ahead." *U.N. World
  Population Conference 19-30 August 1974*, Conference Background Paper
  (E/Conf. 60/CBP/19, 22 March 1974).

Browning, H. L. "Migrant Selectivity and the Growth of Large Cities in Developing
  Countries." *Rapid Population Growth*, Vol. II (National Academy of Sciences).
  Baltimore: The Johns Hopkins Press, 1971.

Buck, P. W. *The Politics of Mercantilism*. New York: Octagon Books, 1964.

Buer, M. C. *Health, Wealth and Population in the Early Days of the Industrial Revolution*. London: Routledge, 1926.

Calhoun, J. B. "Population Density and Social Pathology." In *Population in Perspective*. Edited by L. B. Young. New York: Oxford University Press, 1968.

Calverton, V. F., and Schmalhausen, S. E., eds. *Sex in Civilization*. New York: Garden
  City Publishing Co., 1929.

Carr-Saunders, A. M. *World Population, Past and Present Trends*. Oxford:Clarendon
  Press, 1936.

Carstairs, G. M. "Stress in Human Populations." In *The World's Population*. Edited
  by O. H. Stanford. New York: Oxford University Press, 1972.

Cloud, P. "Mineral Resources in Fact and Fancy." In *Environment, Resources, Pollution and Society*. Edited by W. W. Murdoch. Stanford: Sinauer Associates,
  1971.

Commission on Population Growth and the American Future. *Population and the American Future.* Washington, D.C., 1972.

The Committee on Resources and Man. *Resources and Man.* San Francisco: W. H. Freeman, 1969.

Commoner, B., et al. "The Causes of Pollution." *Environment,* Vol. XIII (April 1971).

Crocker, T. D., and Rogers, A. J., III. *Environmental Economics.* Hinsdale, Ill.: Dryden Press, 1971.

Crocker, W. R. *The Japanese Population Problem.* New York: Macmillan, 1931.

Dales, J. H. *Pollution, Property and Prices.* Toronto: University of Toronto Press, 1968.

Davis, K. "Population Policy: Will Current Programs Succeed?" *Science,* Vol. CLVIII (November 1967).

Davis, K. "The Urbanization of the Human Population." *Scientific American,* Vol. CCXIII (September 1965).

Davis, K. "The World Demographic Transition." *Annals of the American Academy of Political and Social Science,* Vol. CCLXXIII (January 1945).

Davis, K. "The World's Population Crisis." In *Contemporary Social Problems.* Edited by R. K. Merton and R. Nisbet. New York: 1971.

Davis, K. "Zero Population Growth: The Goal and the Means." In *The No-Growth Society.* Edited by M. Olson and H. H. Landsberg. New York; W. W. Norton, 1973.

Davoll, J. "Resources, Renewable and Non-Renewable." In *Resources and Population.* Edited by B. Benjamin et al. London: Academic Press, 1973.

Djerassi, C. "Birth Control after 1984: A Realistic Appraisal of Future Contraceptive Developments." *Are Our Descendants Doomed?* Edited by H. Brown and E. Hutchings. New York: Viking Press, 1970.

Dore, R. P. *Land Reform in Japan.* London: Oxford University Press, 1959.

Dunham, K. "The Influence of Crustal Resources." *Ambio,* Vol. III (1974).

Durand, J. D. "The Modern Expansion of World Population." In *Population and Society.* Edited by C. B. Nam. Boston: Houghton Mifflin Co., 1968.

Dyson, F. J. "Energy in the Universe." *Scientific American,* Vol. CCXXIV (September 1971).

Edel, M. *Economies and the Environment.* Englewood Cliffs, N.J.: Prentice-Hall, 1973.

Ehrlich, P. R. "Controlling World Population." *Current,* June 1968.

Ehrlich, P. R. *The Population Bomb.* New York: Ballantine Books, 1968.

Ehrlich, P. R., and Ehrlich, A. H. *Population, Resources, Environment.* San Francisco: W. H. Freeman, 1970.

Enke, S. "The Economic Case for Birth Control." *Challenge,* May-June 1967.

Enke, S. "Economic Consequences of Rapid Population Growth." *The Economic Journal,* Vol. CXXXI (December 1971).

Enke, S. "High Fertility Impairs Credit Worthiness of Developing Nations." In *Spatial, Regional and Population Economics: Essays in Honour of Edgar M. Hoover.* Edited by M. Perlman et al. New York: Gordon and Breach, 1972.

Finch, B. E. *Contraception through the Ages.* Springfield: C. C. Thomas, 1963.

Flugel, J. C. *Population, Psychology and Peace.* London: Watts, 1947.

Forrester, J. W. "Counterintuitive Behavior of Social Systems." In *Toward Global Equilibrium*. Edited by D. L. Meadows and D. H. Meadows. Cambridge, Mass.: Wright-Allen Press, 1973.

Freedman, J. L. "The Effects of Population Density on Humans." *Psychological Perspectives on Population*. New York: Basic Books, 1973.

Gini, C. *Le rôle du facteur démographique dans la politique internationale*. Bucharest: Centre de Hautes Etudes, n. d.

Green, S. *The Curious History of Contraception*. London: Ebury Press, 1971.

Hartley, S. F. *Population Quantity vs. Quality*. Englewood Cliffs, N.J.: Prentice-Hall, 1972.

Hauser, P. M. "The Chaotic Society: Product of the Social Morphological Revolution." *American Sociological Review*, Vol. XXXIV (February 1969).

Hauser, P. M. "Implications for Economic Development of World Geographic Distribution and Urbanization." Unpublished paper presented at the United Nations Symposium on Population and Development, Cairo, June 4-14, 1973.

Hauser, P. M. "On Non-Family Planning Methods of Population Control." In *Studies in Demography*. Edited by A. Bose et al. Chapel Hill: University of North Carolina Press, 1970.

Hauser, P. M. "Population Criteria in Foreign Aid Programs." Paper prepared for the National Consultation on Ethics and Population Policies, Annapolis, Maryland, May 24-27, 1972.

Hicks, J. R. *The Social Framework*. 4th ed. Oxford: Clarendon Press, 1971.

Himes, N. E. *Medical History of Contraception*. New York: Schocken Books, 1970.

Hoffman, L. W., and Hoffman, M. L. "The Value of Children to Parents." In *Psychological Perspectives on Population*. Edited by J. T. Fawcett. New York: Basic Books, 1973.

Holdren, J., and Herrera, P. *Energy*. New York: Sierra Club, 1971.

Hubbert, M. K. "Energy Resources." *Environment, Resources, Pollution and Society*. Edited by W. W. Murdoch. Stanford: Sinauer Associates, 1971.

Hubbert, M. K. "The Energy Resources of the Earth." *Scientific American*, Vol. CCXXIV (September 1971).

Hutber, F. W., and Forster, C. I. K. "Sources of Energy and Their Adequacy for Man's Needs." In *Resources and Population*. Edited by B. Benjamin et al. London: Academic Press, 1927.

Kangas, L. W. "Integrated Incentives for Fertility Control." *Science*, Vol. CLXIX.

Kneese, A. V. "Background for the Economic Analysis of Environmental Pollution." *The Swedish Journal of Economics*, Vol. LXXIII (March 1971).

Kuznets, S. *Population, Capital and Growth*. New York: W. W. Norton, 1973.

Landsberg, H. H. "Low-Cost, Abundant Energy: Paradise Lost?" *Science*, Vol. LXXXIV (April 1974).

Leibenstein, H. *Economic Backwardness and Economic Growth*. New York: John Wiley, 1957.

Lenin, V. I. "Theory of the Agrarian Question." *V. I. Lenin Selected Works*, Vol. XII. New York: International Publishers, 1938.

Luten, D. B. "The Economic Geography of Energy." *Scientific American*, Vol. CCXXIV (September 1971).

Meade, J. E. "Economic Policy and the Threat of Doom." In *Resources and Population*. Edited by B. Benjamin et al. London: Academic Press, 1973.

Meadows, D. L. "Introduction to the Project." In *Toward Global Equilibrium*. Edited by D. L. Meadows and D. H. Meadows. Cambridge, Mass.: Wright-Allen Press, 1973.

Meadows, D. H., et al. *The Limits to Growth*. New York: Universe Books, 1972.

Moller, H. "Youth as a Force in the Modern World." *Comparative Studies in Society and History*, Vol. X (April 1968).

Nam, C. B., ed. *Population and Society*. Boston: Houghton Mifflin, 1968.

Oltmans, W. L. *On Growth*. New York: C. P. Putnam's Sons, 1974.

Overbeek, J. *History of Population Theories*. Rotterdam: Rotterdam University Press, 1974.

Paddock, W., and Paddock, P. *Famine 1975*. Boston: Little, Brown and Co., 1967.

Petersen, W. *The Politics of Population*. London: V. Gollanes, 1964.

Pitchford, J. D. *The Economics of Population: An Introduction*. Canberra: Australian National University Press, 1974.

Pohlman, E. *The Psychology of Birth Planning*. Cambridge, Mass.: Schenkman, 1969.

Population Council. "World Population Status Report 1974." *Reports on Population/ Family Planning*, No. 15 (January 1974).

Rainwater, *And the Poor Get Children*. Chicago: Quadrangle Books, 1960.

Revelle, R., et al., eds. *The Survival Equation*. New York: Houghton Mifflin, 1971.

Ridker, R. G. "The Impact of Population Growth on Resources and the Environment." *Towards the End of Growth*. Englewood Cliffs, N.J.: Prentice-Hall, 1973.

Ridker, R. G. "Synopsis of a Proposal for a Family Planning Bond." *Studies in Family Planning*, June 1969.

Rose, D. J. "Energy Policy in the U.S." *Scientific American*, Vol. CCXXX (January 1974).

Ruthenberg, H. "The World Food Problem." *Economics*, Vol. V (1972).

Samuel, T. J. "The Strengthening of the Motivation for Family Limitation in India." *The Journal of Family Welfare*, Vol. XIII (December 1966).

Schearer, S. B. "To-morrow's Contraception." In *Toward the End of Growth*. Edited by C. F. Westoff et al. Englewood Cliffs, N.J.: Prentice-Hall, 1973.

Scientific American. *The Human Population*. San Francisco: W. H. Freeman, 1974.

Segal, S. J., and Tietse, C. "Contraceptive Technology: Current and Prospective Methods." *Reports on Population/Family Planning*, July 1971.

Simon, J. L. *The Effects of Income on Fertility*. Chapel Hill, N.C.: Caroline Population Center, Monograph 19, 1974.

Simon, J. L. "The Role of Bonuses and Persuasive Propaganda in the Reduction of Birth Rates." *Economic Development and Cultural Change*, Vol. XVI (April 1968).

Spengler, J. J. *Population Economics*. Durham, N.C.: Duke University Press, 1972.

Spengler, J. J. "Population Problem, In Search of a Solution." *Science*, Vol. CLXVI (December 1969).

Spengler, J. J. "World Hunger: Past, Present, Prospective . . ." *World Review of Nutrition and Dietetics*, Vol. IX (1968).

Stycos, J. M. *Family Planning and Fertility in Puerto Rico*. New York: Columbia University Press, 1955.

Stycos, J. M. *Ideology, Faith and Family Planning in Latin America.* New York: McGraw-Hill, 1971.

Sweezy, A. R. "Population, GNP and the Environment." In *Are Our Descendants Doomed?* Edited by H. Brown and E. Hutchings. New York: Viking Press, 1972.

United Nations, Department of Economic and Social Affairs, *The Determinants and Consequences of Population Trends.* (St. SOA/SER. A/50). New York, 1973.

U.S. Congress, House, Committee on Merchant Marine and Fisheries. *Growth and Its Implications for the Future,* Hearing Before the subcommittee on Fisheries and Wildlife Conservation and the Environment, House of Representatives, 93rd Cong., 1st sess., 1973.

Westoff, C. F. "Changes in Contraceptive Practices among Married Couples." In *Toward the End of Growth.* Edited by C. F. Westoff et al. Englewood Cliffs, N.J.: Prentice-Hall, 1973.

Wright, F. C. *Population and Peace.* Paris: International Institute of Intellectual Co-operation, 1934.

Zimmerman, A. *Catholic Viewpoint on Overpopulation.* New York: Hanover House, 1961.

Index

About the Author

Johannes Overbeek, associate professor of economics at the University of Guelph, Canada, is a specialist in the economics of population change and population policy. After receiving his Ph.D. from the University of Geneva, Professor Overbeek taught at the University of British Columbia and the University of Hawaii, where he was a research associate at the East-West Population Institute. He has written primarily on the history of population theory.